PAWN ON A CHESSBOARD

Mary Porter-Truax

TATE PUBLISHING, LLC

Published in the United States of America
by Tate Publishing, LLC
127 East Trade Center Terrace
Mustang, OK 73064
(888) 361–9473

ISBN: 1-5988635-7-6

DEDICATION AND
ACKNOWLEDGEMENTS

"Pawn on a Chessboard" is dedicated to the memory of my saintly Aunt Minnie F. Truax, even though she will never know I kept my promise to her that one day I would indeed author a book under the name of "Truax" and bring recognition to the family name.

Without the able assistance and enthusiastic support of Ms. Judy Reynolds and Mr. Don Castillo, graphic artist par excellence, "Pawn on a Chessboard" would still be only a dream gathering dust on my closet shelf. When my health deteriorated to the point where I could not get around to do the myriad of things entailed in getting a book into print, Judy and Don pitched in and did the job for me; all the time making it sound as though I was doing them a favor in allowing them to do so.

Judy typed the manuscript, searched the Internet to find a publisher who might be interested in a book of this kind, obtained the copyright, and thought of the tantalizing caption at the bottom of the front cover. Don designed the imaginative and beautifully appropriate cover, utilizing scenes and events from the book as described to him by Judy. Don also took my picture and arranged for an artist to draw a rendering appropriate for the back of my book. I can never thank them enough for their efforts.

I would also like to express my appreciation to Laurie Buckley for the really great job she did on the chapter headings and the lovely foreword she wrote. Laurie is a writer, and as one can see, a very good writer.

CONTENTS

INTRODUCTION

The fact that "Pawn on a Chessboard" was written in answer to the question, "How do people survive out there?" (on the street), does not mean that this book is anything like an exhaustive expose of survival on the street. Pawn is rather the story of how one group of people survived this kind of an existence for several years.

Catholic Charities of Las Vegas, Nevada, deserves so much appreciation for their establishment and maintenance of St. Vincent's Plaza. St. Vincent's was originally a shopping center known as Vegas Village. Sometime after Vegas Village closed its doors forever, Catholic Charities acquired the property and remodeled the building to serve as their offices: a homeless shelter for men, a soup kitchen, and other enterprises.

A large area on the north side of the building was fenced off, and roofing was erected along the fence on three sides of this quadrangle. This was the "yard" where so much of the action in this book took place.

FOREWORD

Living in the world's richest country, it's hard to believe that the condition of America's homeless could be in such disarray. We have developed the technology for space travel and yet have chosen not to find a way to embrace their pathetic conditions and resolve them.

If there were hundreds of thousands of Americans tragically trapped by some immediate circumstance, as a nation we would be outraged and demand they be rescued. Today we are dealing with hundreds of thousands of invisible homeless Americans, individually trapped by circumstance, and a nation still not angry enough to demand a permanent solution. Over the last several years, there has been a small, steady momentum from cities to grassroots organizations to implement programs that will actually help these forgotten Americans out of their despair.

"Pawn on a Chessboard" is a remarkable insight to what this movement is trying to accomplish and how important it is to rescue these people. Through the eyes of a woman who is about to enjoy her retirement years, we get a chance to see into the fascinating, frightening, and sometimes humorous world of homeless Americans.

Mary Porter-Truax tells an amazing story about her journey into homelessness and how she survived for over twenty of her golden years in the desert wilderness, the streets, and various shelters of Las Vegas, Nevada. In the shadows of the entertainment capital of the world, with millions of visitors every year and revenues in the billions, she fell into despair and found herself living with no home, a shopping cart, and a few personal belongings. Mary takes us gently by the hand and walks us through the lonely, harsh reality of a place none of us would want to belong. It is a place where people are arrested for being poor, veterans are forgotten, city officials turn their backs, and the image of their misfortune is used against them. As her story unfolds, she has a marvelous way of making you feel like you are right there with her. With a graciousness all her own, she interprets her circumstances with an honesty and humor that allows the reader to trust her observations and her invaluable instincts for understanding what is happening. She explains the social services for the homeless—how they work and how they fail—and the things they really need to help them.

Like a reporter on the wild side, Mary gives an unselfish observation of the tribal living that goes on, how people band together in little communities, and how she protected herself. The genuine friendships she made are touching, charming, and heartwarming. She puts names and faces on real Americans, and talks about what brought them there, as well as how they dealt with it.

Dealing with extreme temperatures (120 degrees to freezing), windstorms, poor vision and approaching age, she was compelled to rise above her circumstance and document. Mary was so touched by the level of humanity she discovered along the way that she began to write a journal about these marvelous people and her adventures. As a first time author, Mary had always had a love for writing. She could have never dreamed how much that would serve her in the twilight of her years.

"Pawn on a Chessboard" is a gift to America, and a chance to walk in the shoes of our forgotten citizens who cry out to be remembered and deserve to be heard.

Laurie Buckley
Host of Bits & Pieces
Starstruck Radio KNEWS
970AM and Internet

CHAPTER 1
HALF-PAST JUPITER AND A QUARTER-PAST VENUS

"*Yooo hooo!*" The call of St. Vincent's early morning hoot owl echoed across the field of sleeping people. It was approximately ten minutes to five in the morning, and Hootie was at his self-imposed task of awakening the drowsy campers before the Las Vegas police (better known as "Metro") made their morning rounds. Anyone in these camps after daybreak stood a good chance of going to jail—not the happiest way to start one's day.

A black man in his early fifties, Hootie was charming, peripatetic and totally irrepressible. He seemed to be much younger than his chronological age would indicate. His real name is Hughie, as were his fathers and his paternal grandfathers before him. An only child and a devoted son, Hughie worked two jobs and spent his life savings taking care of his mother during her last illness. His father had passed away quite sometime before his mother died.

Although he was not caught in the early morning surprise raid when twenty-three of us were picked up, Hughie had decided to devote his pre-dawn hours to preventing a recurrence of this mishap. Much to his dismay, early-rising Hughie had actually witnessed the whole arrest scene from his balcony.

He had been living outdoors for a while, and he knew us at the time of the arrests. Hughie had a job and was living in an apartment near St. Vincent's Plaza, which was also by the campsite. This site was located across Foremaster Lane from St. Vincent's.

Even before we were out of jail, however, he had

decided to move back to the yard, in spite of the fact he was still working. He never did tell me his reason for moving. I knew that the apartment house where he lived did not have a very good reputation for upkeep, and Hughie was a meticulously clean person.

Some ungrateful souls grumbled at being awakened so early, but no one needed to oversleep and go to jail unless they wanted to do so. I certainly did not want to, so I was usually awake even before our kindly chanticleer sounded his morning reveille. Due to the illuminating lights from surrounding streetlamps, the field was not completely dark, but was dark enough that I could not see my watch. I had learned to tell time by the planets.

When it is half-past Jupiter and quarter past Venus planetary time, I knew it was a quarter to five our time. So when Venus appeared to be four feet above the roof of the grocery store, which formed the eastern boundary of the field, and Jupiter was already well on his way across the morning sky, I'd better be up and moving.

On cloudy nights when the planets were not visible, I had to get up the first time I woke up and go to one of the streetlights to check my watch, or trust that Hughie would not oversleep that morning. The grocery store management wanted us out of the field by 5:15 a.m. That was when the huge produce trucks started delivering their merchandise.

The storeowners worried that seeing us would embarrass the truck drivers. I seriously doubted that the psyche of most truck drivers was all that fragile. I couldn't understand why the truck drivers would have been embarrassed to see our homelessness. I should think it would be the other way around. Be that as it may, 5:15 a.m. became the deadline for our being out of the field.

At that time, we were not allowed on St. Vincent's

property until 5:30 a.m. I used to park myself and my cart beside a mesquite bush near the highway and wait there until 5:30 a.m. Then I could cross Main Street to St. Vincent's west side parking lot. We all waited in the parking lot until the fenced-in yard was cleared and we could get in for the day, usually around 7:30 a.m. Without daily access to St. Vincent's, I don't know what some of us would have done without the yard to stay in. I guess we probably would have spent most of our time in the Las Vegas City Jail.

One chilly morning, I was sitting on my overturned bucket beside my friendly bush when I saw my friends, Allie and Archie, coming down the path toward the highway. Allie was a plumpish, vivacious and attractive white lady in her early fifties. Archie, who was also vivacious, was a very witty black man in his early sixties. They were a really cute couple.

Allie and I had met in 1978, when we stayed at the Triple A Hotel in downtown Las Vegas. The Triple A was actually a flophouse, but it was kept reasonably clean and the bedding was changed weekly, unless someone moved out. One room, in back of the office, was reserved for women.

Allie was originally from Florida. Divorced and with her children grown, she worked until she got a stake. Then she would come to Las Vegas and have a ball spending it. At the time we met, she had gone broke again. This time she got a job at the Lady Luck Casino and came to the Triple A to live. I was already staying there, and we soon became friends.

As neither of us could afford a better room or an apartment by ourselves, we decided to find a place we could share. Allie was awaiting her first paycheck, and I was waiting for my next pension check, when she came home from work one day, bubbling over with enthusiasm. "Mary!" she exclaimed excitedly, "I found a place we can afford. It's called the MacDonald Hotel, and it is only fifty dollars a week."

I could not bear to tell her that the MacDonald Hotel was a hangout for most of the hookers in downtown Las Vegas. We really wanted to get out of the flophouse and could afford the rent, so we decided to take a chance on the MacDonald. If we did not like it, we could always save our money and look for something else.

When we got our respective checks, there was a room available at the MacDonald, so we moved into the hotel. The bathroom was down the hall, and it was a little dingy, but the room and the bedding were kept clean, and we had twin beds. Surprisingly enough, the place was not noisy, and neither the girls nor their patrons ever bothered us.

Since Allie worked nights, I spent most of my days playing the penny slots at the old Club Bingo on Fremont Street. We didn't get in each other's way, and we each lived our own life. Eventually, Allie had a job offer that would pay her more than the casino job did. I thought I had a job, with an apartment attached, lined up in North Las Vegas. Allie and I parted company amicably. Neither of our jobs worked out, but that was another story.

Now, some ten years or so later and quite by coincidence, we were both living on the street. The MacDonald Hotel, which was chronically plagued with fires, eventually burned down, and the Triple A Hotel went out of business.

Archie and Allie had met when they were on the street at the same time. They fell in love and a year later, they were married.

One morning, in the semi-darkness and with my

nearsightedness, I could dimly see Allie. All I could see of Archie was the white blanket draped around his shoulders. When my friends got close enough to hear me, I called out brightly, "I see two ghosts coming down the path . . . no, a ghost and a half!"

Not stopping for one moment to think, Archie answered, "Yes, I haven't been taking my vitamins, and I'm fading."

Hughie and Archie were not at all sensitive about their color. If they had been, I wouldn't have dreamt of mentioning it. In fact, it was Archie who told me the first summer I was out here that if I got any darker, they would have to start calling me "*sistuh*." Archie was from Philadelphia, and sometimes his "r's" tended to get lost in the translation.

One morning, when some of us were still camped across Foremaster Lane from St. Vincent's, we jumped the gun a little and got to the lot about fifteen minutes early. Most of us stayed up by the curb, barely on St. Vincent's property, if indeed we were on their property. We were close enough to make the St. Vincent's security guard very nervous, and he asked us to move off the property before he got chewed out by his boss.

That was all right with me and one other woman, so we prepared to move our carts back across the street. For some reason, the rest of our companions refused to move. Someone called for Hughie. I started to leave because I'd had a long history of running away whenever trouble loomed on the horizon. This time I decided to be brave and stand my ground with my companions, even if I did think we were being a little silly. As it turned out, we were being quite a bit silly. A heated altercation ensued between Hughie and the guard, in the course of which the rattled guard threatened to call the police. He must have had a tough boss.

Anyway, Hughie told him to go ahead and call the police, while Janie and I clung to our carts and muttered, "No Hughie, no Hughie." But Hughie did, and so did the guard. All this for only fifteen minutes? Perhaps more than just those fifteen minutes were involved in this little tempest in a teacup. Maybe it was a rebellion taking a spontaneous stand against what some people thought of as an unreasonable regulation, which caused unnecessary hardship for the homeless.

Whatever it was, foolishness or some sort of desperate rebellion, two Metro patrol cars pulled up, flashing those official-looking lights on our huddled little group. I was little more than a mass of quivering jelly and wishing I was anywhere but there. I had pulled my cart over to the curb, reasoning that if cars could park there, then a shopping cart should have the same privilege, and I was not on St. Vincent's property.

The officers pointed out the fact that by that time, we had only ten more minutes to wait, so would we please go back across the street and do our waiting there? By that time, I had used up my small store of courage. I was so relieved not to find myself in manacles and on the way to jail that I gladly led the parade back across Foremaster Lane. That was the last time I tried to be brave, especially in the face of someone's threat to call the police. They might have meant what they said.

Eventually, the powers that be at St. Vincent's relaxed the rules a bit, and we were allowed on the property at 4:00 a.m. This made life a little less nerve-racking for us. It gave us a chance to be out of our camps by daylight, and less chance of being picked up by the police.

Early in the summer of 1988, I resolved to resign myself to living on the street for a few more months, saving my money, and eventually getting a room or an apartment. The catch was that when I used up my savings, I would probably find myself back on the street, but I decided not to worry about that. In the meantime, I would apply for low-cost housing and perhaps get something going before my money ran out.

Life, however, had another idea for me. On the morning of Saturday, July 23rd of that year, while camped on the same hill across from Foremaster Lane, I found myself in handcuffs and on the way to jail for the first time in my seventy-six years. As if poverty itself was not enough of a prison.

I was usually up and out of camp before daylight. But on that morning, for some unknown reason, I had overslept by only a few minutes, but it was just enough.

By the time I had loaded my plastic and bedding into my cart and was about to start down the driveway, yesterday's fallen night had already shattered into luminous shards of a new day. I was too late. I was just starting to push my cart down the hill when somebody said, "*Police!*" No, dear Lord, don't let it be the police. Maybe they were just paying us a friendly visit. But it was the police, and they were not at all that friendly.

I started to pass the paddy wagon with my shopping cart and tried to look as innocent and inconspicuous as possible. As I was pushing all of my earthly possessions off someone else's property at the crack of dawn, I heard the brusque command, "Park the cart and drop your bag!" (He was referring to the plastic shopping bag in which I carried my purse to keep it clean and undamaged.) No doubt about it, the police were speaking to me.

I suppose there are comparable sensations to the panic I felt at that moment; sensations such as the sinking feeling of helpless inevitability that sweeps over one when one's car stalls on the freeway in rush-hour traffic.

Or it might be the "Oh, Lord, not again!" routine that one has when that idiotic doctor leans back in his chair and says fatuously, "Congratulations, Mrs. Doe. In eight more months, you will be the mother of a beautiful baby." All this when you haven't had a decent night's sleep since you had your last beautiful baby. Well, that was not your last one, obviously; you did the wrong thing for that.

That morning's surprise raid had been the result of a complaint filed against us by some of the neighboring property owners. I could not blame them. The whole lower area on the west side of the field, along the fence by the produce store, looked like a city dump or worse. Some of us would come and go during the hours of darkness, destroy no property, and would self-destruct before we would ever litter. But unfortunately, not all transients are that conscientious.

They were the ones who caused problems for the rest of us and for the property owners who were kind enough to allow us to camp on their premises. The mess, much of which constituted a fire hazard, jeopardized the insurance on some of these properties. The owners were finally forced to take action. The joke of the arrest situation was that all of us, who were picked up that morning, were not the worst of the offenders. I don't know where those people were that day. However, since the police had neither the time nor the means to ascertain who was innocent and who was guilty, they swept us all in, treating innocent and guilty alike.

CHAPTER 2
GOING TO JAIL FOR BEING POOR

We filled the paddy wagon and several patrol cars. In fact, we overfilled the paddy wagon and my friend Greta had to sit on Ferdie's legs all the way to City Hall. Although not huge, Greta was solid. By the time we reached our destination, poor Ferdie's legs were paralyzed. Manacled as Ferdie was, and Greta with only one arm, they could not shift to a more comfortable position.

I was fortunate enough to be one of the first of our group to be arrested and was cuffed with some of the old fashioned metal handcuffs. Some of my companions were not so lucky, and their wrists were taped. These plastic tapes are miserable devices that are put on so tightly that they have to be cut off by the detention officers at the jail. No matter how careful the officers tried to be, people's wrists were left raw and bleeding. I did not see anyone receiving medical treatment for those wounds, but perhaps I was in error. I hope so.

Once we got to the City Jail, we were unmanacled and made to stand spread-eagle against a wall while we were searched for weapons and/or drugs, I suppose. The female officer who searched me announced that I was "clean," but she did not say what I was clean of. This spread-eagle position was a very undignified position to be placed in. If I hadn't been so determined to write this book, I would have given up right then. Reliving those humiliating experiences over and over again hasn't been much fun. But I had started writing and I was determined to finish it even if it killed me, which it probably wouldn't. It would just have to embarrass me for the rest of my life.

Upon the completion of the search, we were taken to the drunk tank, although none of us had been drinking. That morning's roundup had netted what were probably some of the mildest, most inoffensive and harmless transients in all of Vegas.

The holding room was a very small room about 25'x25.' There was a bench that seated five or six women along one wall with a toilet and washbowl on another wall. At the time we were taken in, there were not many women in the tank, and I was able to get a place on the bench. Metro must have been busy the rest of the day because the little room was rapidly filling up. There was no clock in sight and no windows, and we had not been allowed to keep our wristwatches, so we had no idea what time it was. Eventually, I became so tired that I couldn't sit up one more minute. I found a place to lie down on the floor, which wasn't clean. Still the women poured in, until finally there was barely standing room. I squeezed against the wall as tightly as I could in order to make room for the newcomers, but I could not have stood up to save my life. I felt so sorry for the ones who had to stand all those hours.

I didn't know how long we were kept in those miserable circumstances. Twenty-four hours was the usual time for this part of the incarceration. There was little else to do, and the women became tired and understandably upset. A number of arguments erupted among them. One notorious troublemaker, who came in some time after we did, had to be put in solitary confinement because she started so many fights. She might have been drinking before her arrest; I had heard rumors that she sometimes did tipple.

Eventually, we were taken to the jail's delousing center, whether we needed debugging or not. I had heard about this process and did not look forward to the experience with any great amount of joy. As the procedure was somewhat personal, I will not go into the details here. The female officer, who conducted this ritual, really was a lady. She did not make us feel embarrassed or treat us like trash, although I imagine she had had her share of unpleasant encounters with some of the city's guests that are more obnoxious. She kidded me about being so fast at disrobing when she requested us to do so. I told her just to call me "Speedy," and she laughed. She was a lovely person.

Besides my sister street women, most of the other female prisoners at that time were young black prostitutes—"whores" they called themselves, without shame. That was simply their profession. Some of them called me "Mom" and asked if they could have any food that I did not want. We were given three big meals a day, catered and brought in on trays. I was not getting enough exercise to work off all those calories, so I usually had something for them.

As I mentioned, the police must have been busy that weekend because the cellblock we were transferred to was literally overflowing. There were five cells, with four bunks in each cell. All the bunks were filled, and some of us, the lucky ones, slept on plastic mats on the floor. Others slept on the floor without mats, while others stretched out on tables in the dining/recreation room. One woman even slept on the floor in the shower/toilet room.

The floors, at the Stewart Street downtown jail, were not carpeted as they were said to be at the Stewart and Mojave Street jail. The prisoners had to clean the cellblocks. They were bribed into it with between-meal snacks, which they did not get until the job was completed. The Stewart and Mojave detention center was known to the experienced as the Country Club. I took their word for it, because anything at all was better than the downtown jail. However, whoever said that a turn in the clink was supposed to be enjoyable?

This experience was supposed to make us repent our sins, not enjoy them, and the downtown pokey was designed to do that, all right. I chose long ago to repent the eighth deadly sin, poverty. That repentance, sincere as it was, did not prevent my going to jail for being poor. That was not the formal charge against me, of course. When I finally got to see the complaint against me, it said something like, " .. . . . loitering on somebody else's property, thereby embarrassing the City of Las Vegas." I don't know why my loitering on somebody else's property should embarrass Las Vegas. I guess that the homeless easily embarrassed cities, like truck drivers.

Finally, I was taken back to the receiving area where I was mugged and fingerprinted. At last, I had a police record. I was in despair! Why hadn't my parents gone fishing instead on the day they conceived me? It was a question they must have frequently asked themselves before they passed away in their eighties. The two officers, one male and one female, who performed this induction routine were a little brusque at first. When they found me to be a cooperative subject, however, and when I assured them that I had not messed up my life on purpose, their attitude thawed considerably and we parted on a cordial note.

The detention officers do have their problems. One woman, who had been picked up some time after we were, beat up on one of the female detention officers before she could be stopped. She did not appear to be on booze or drugs and was quite friendly to the other prisoners when she got to the cellblock. I guess she just did not want to go to jail. She, too, had been picked up for sleeping in the wrong place.

I did not ask to look at my mug shots. If the picture ID I carried with me was any criterion, the fingerprints were better looking than the photographs. I never was very photogenic, and age had not improved that condition. I had two thoughts about my picture ID. On the one hand, it better look like me or I was in trouble. On the other hand, it was so terrible that every time someone said, "Yes, that's you all right," I thought, "Oh, my lord, do I really look that bad?" I guess I did.

Because the nurse had not been on duty over the weekend, the jail nurse examined us. This examination consisted of taking our blood pressure and asking some questions about our medical history and personal habits.

No, I had not had this, that, or the other disease.

No, I wasn't on any kind of medication except over-the-counter pain pills for headaches and arthritis.

No, I didn't use alcohol or drugs.

At the last answer, the nurse looked at me sharply, as though doubting my veracity. Didn't she know that people got put in jail just for sleeping in the wrong place? They didn't have to be drunk and disorderly in order to attract Metro's attention. But then I suppose she had been lied to a lot. Despite my age and the stress I was under, my blood pressure was only 120/70. The nurse could not doubt the evidence of her own instruments, and I got an approving, "That's good," on that one.

For years I had read stories and seen movies about prostitutes and their pimps. Now, I was seeing some of these young ladies close up. I was shocked to learn that they actually believed their pimps had the right to beat them if they chanced to offend those kindly gentlemen. Had they ever been brainwashed! The saddest part of this situation was that it was highly unlikely that these women would ever know any other kind of life. I felt so sorry for them. They were so very young, and they did not feel sorry for themselves. Perhaps that was sad, too.

The maximum period of time for which arrestees were supposed to be held without being charged with something was seventy-two hours. Weekends, however, were not counted in this time. Since we were picked up on a Saturday morning, this last fact meant that over seventy-two hours would extend to the following Thursday morning. On Wednesday morning, some of us finally had our day in court. At last we would be told what the charges were against us.

The small courtroom was a room not far from the cellblocks. It contained a few benches, a television set with a camera on top of it (real-life Court TV), and a small table. The police officer, who presided over our end of the proceedings, sat there with his papers. This was not at all reminiscent of Perry Mason or Matlock, and I wondered if I really was in a court of law. The judge must have been seated at the other end of the television circuit, because we could hear him, but we couldn't see him.

As we sat on the benches, waiting our turn in front of the television set and the camera, the officer was talking with some of the women. Most of them seemed to know him. I hadn't been paying much attention to their conversation, until I heard the officer say that he was a male chauvinist. Without thinking where I was or who he was, I blurted out an involuntary, "Oh, boy!" Up to that time, Officer Bob had not seemed to notice that I was on the scene. I should have left well enough alone. For that bit of irreverence, I received a stare from him that was so long and so cold that I didn't think I ever wanted to meet him again; not under the same kind of circumstances anyway. I had the uncomfortable feeling that if Officer Bob had been the judge that day, I would have spent the rest of my life in the Las Vegas City Jail with no hope of parole—ever!

Since the arrest, I had been practicing saying, "Your honor," with the proper deference. But when my name was called, I leaped from the bench to take my place before the television set and the camera. All that came out was a rather small, "Yes, sir." While we were awaiting our trial, we had been given copies of the complaint against us. The judge must have been satisfied with the "Yes, sir," because his voice was quite kindly. He explained to me that if I chose to plead guilty to the charges against me, I would get off with time served. Getting off with time served meant that the time already spent in jail had satisfied one's debt to society, and one could once again become a respectable member of the community.

I was both happy and relieved to do that. I had half expected to be given a later court date and a fine to pay. That sometimes happened. The very thought panicked me. I could not afford a fine, or so I thought. I already owed some back taxes to the federal government, and between the IRS and the City of Las Vegas, I could just see myself spending the rest of my life in debtor's prison. That was my usual optimism at work, of course.

I had to wait until afternoon for my release, as I was one of the last of our group to be freed. We were given the paper sacks containing our possessions. The only possessions I had were the clothes I was wearing when I was picked up, as the arresting officer had not allowed me to bring even my wallet, containing my money and ID, to jail with me. Both the shopping bag and my purse had been left sitting in the driveway where I was ordered to drop them.

Fortunately for my peace of mind, I found out from one of my sister prisoners, who had called St. Vincent's and talked to Margaret, that Hughie had rescued both my cart and my purse and was taking care of them for me. I heard later that since that time, arresting officers were required to allow arrestees to take their purses and/or small bags to jail with them. Greta had not been allowed to take her backpack, which contained vital medication with her. Medication had been provided for her at the jail. However, I don't know how they got her prescription, but fortunately for her they came up with something.

My clothes were clean at the time of our arrest, but after lying for hours on the holding room floor, they were no longer so clean. Not only that, but the paper sacks containing our possessions had somehow gotten into some water. Now my clothes were both dirty and wet, but at that moment they were all I had. Due to the early hour at which we had been picked up, those were not the clothes I would normally have worn to town to begin with. I had always tried to keep at least two presentable looking outfits to wear outside the yard, but the police had not given us time to change our clothes.

The Las Vegas City Hall was a confusing place to find one's way out of, and we had not been given the cook's tour of the building. Although an officer escorted us to the first floor, I left from the Stewart Street exit and made what I thought was the right hand turn that would have taken me along Stewart to north Main Street and home. Instead, I found myself walking for two more blocks without seeing anything resembling the buildings on that stretch of Stewart Street. I was unable to recognize any buildings, and I hadn't remembered any of them being on that stretch of Las Vegas Boulevard. I began to wonder how I had managed to get there.

City Hall was at the corner of Stewart Street and Las Vegas Boulevard, so I had obviously walked down Las Vegas Boulevard, but why? Had I come out some exit that I did not know about, or had downtown Las Vegas been turned around while I was out of touch with the world?

I've since checked City Hall for an exit on Las Vegas Boulevard, but have never found one. Had some giant hand turned downtown Las Vegas around? I was the one who was turned around. So now I found myself standing on one of the busiest corners in glamorous downtown Las Vegas with no purse, no money, no ID, but with only the wet, dirty clothes I was wearing. The back of my neck was scraggly and unkempt looking as well. I wore my hair short, so I had to keep my neck shaved. We were given a comb and a washcloth in jail, but not a razor, so I had not been able to keep my neck trimmed.

I was convinced that everyone who saw me had to believe I had just arrived in town on a freight train, especially the police. If only five days in jail had so disoriented me, I could imagine what years in prison must do to people. Worried that I could be picked up again just for looking like a vagrant, I hurriedly retraced my steps back to City Hall. This time I made the turn that would take me to Main Street and home, or what I loosely called home. It was the only home I had, anyway. At that moment it sounded like home and felt like paradise. Things were indeed relative.

Since writing this adventure, I talked to Margaret and found out that there is a back exit to City Hall, which led to Las Vegas Boulevard. In my disorientation on the day of my release, I obviously had not noticed that we did not come through the building lobby and down the steps, which led to Stewart Street. It was a relief to have that mystery cleared up, although I still haven't found that exit. The jail experience was not the worst thing that ever happened to me, but it was still embarrassing enough and trying enough that I did not care to repeat the performance. I have not dared to make a good resolution since that time, lest I bring another unpleasant event down on myself.

Once again, though, I was one of the more fortunate of our group, even though I was one of the last to be released. Some of my friends, and others too, I suppose, were set free in the middle of the night—women as well as men. Not only didn't this make any sense to me, it was cruel. In the first place, many of us were in jail because we had no socially acceptable place to sleep. A more or less extended stay in jail was not a permanent solution to the problem. People still had no place to go at that hour of the night.

St. Vincent's yard was locked at night, and most of the shelters either had early curfews or were filled up by that time. People did not dare go back to the area where they had been picked up, as Metro might still be watching the site. Neither was walking the city streets at that hour of the night considered a safe activity, for either men or women.

As I walked down the Main Street hill toward the yard, I saw Hughie coming up the hill toward me. Knowing that there was no smoking in the Las Vegas City Jail, he offered me a cigarette and escorted me the rest of the way home. As we walked through the yard gate, he called out in his best Hughie voice, "Hey, everybody, look who's here!" Gone were any hopes I might have had to slip inconspicuously into my slot under the arcade roof.

A few people called out perfunctory greetings, mostly to please Hughie I think, but no one bothered to ask the one question that was practically mandatory on these occasions: namely, "What kind of a bird doesn't fly?" The answer was, of course, "A jailbird." Some embarrassed souls refuse to say "Jailbird," and say, "A dead bird," instead. But this answer was not exactly appropriate to these circumstances. Not usually anyway.

By this time, however, I was practically beyond embarrassment. I was determined to have my initiation into the Exalted Order of Jailbirds to which my five days as a guest of the City of Las Vegas entitled me. I had paid my dues, now I wanted my reward. I was well on my way to home base, but still the pertinent question did not come. Close to despair, I finally decided to take matters into my own hands. It was something like the impatient Napoleon snatching the crown from the grasp of a probably startled prelate and crowning himself emperor. I asked myself the initiatory question and answered it in the conventionally correct manner.

I really knew I was home, though, when I got to my chair. As I turned to sit down, one of the pinochle players looked up from his game long enough to observe, "Ma Barker is back."

"Yes," I replied, "and now we plan our revenge against Metro."

The man laughed, and of course I was only joking. As said elsewhere, the police were acting on a legitimate complaint, and I bore them no rancor. The next morning in the parking lot, where the multiple arrests were still being discussed, I also learned that I had passed my initiation successfully when one of the men turned to me and said, "Now you are one of us." Apparently there had been some doubt about this before that time. Oh well, everybody needs to belong somewhere.

CHAPTER 3
THE PERILS OF MARY

Looking back, I think that for some time, something or someone had been trying to get me off that hill. I don't recall exactly when they started, but prior to the arrests, I had suffered a series of bizarre accidents in my camp. I used to tie one end of a large piece of plastic to one side of my cart. I would anchor the other end of the plastic to the ground with pieces of cement, which we found lying around the camp area.

That made a cozy little tent, which gave me a measure of privacy and protected me from the elements. One morning, when I was dismantling my camp, I must have tripped over one of the cement pieces. It happened so fast that I did not know what I had done. Suddenly I found myself hurtling headlong down that steep, paved driveway. My fall was violently and painfully halted when my head collided with the handle of my downhill-side neighbor's cart.

The force of the collision nearly knocked Eddie's "house" down and jarred him awake. I guess he thought he had been hit by one of the huge produce trucks that sometimes drove up into the driveway to turn around. I had a lump on my head for several days, but I probably would have had more than a minor lump on the head if I had tumbled clear to the bottom of that long, hard driveway. I don't think that I would ever again laugh at poor little Jack and Jill and their tumble down the hill. I knew then how they must have felt.

Several days after the aforementioned incident, it

was a moderately windy night on the hill when we started to set up our camps. Although I have had my experiences with carts being tipped over by the wind, I decided that night the breeze was not strong enough to give me a problem. So, I put up my little canopy and went to bed. That was not one of the more intelligent decisions of my life.

Some time during the night, the wind increased to gale force gusts. It lifted the plastic from under the anchoring pieces of cement, leaving that end of the canopy to fly wildly and noisily in the wind. I got up to take the tent the rest of the way down. I resigned to sleeping the rest of the night in the open with the wind blowing the covers off me and blowing dirt all over me.

Eddie, however, also awake at that time. Trying to be helpful, he had another idea. He said he had some rocks the wind couldn't disturb, and he was so right. Once again I anchored the plastic to the ground—this time with Eddie's rocks—then went back to bed. True to Eddie's promise, the next strong gust of wind did not blow the plastic from under the rocks.

Instead, it bellied the plastic upward and pulled the heavy cart over onto my head and shoulders, pinning me firmly to my bed. Struggling against the cart, I could not get enough leverage to push that cart off me. Eddie and Bernie, my uphill-side neighbors, noticed my plight and rushed over to lift the cart off me. I suppose if they hadn't, I would have been sprawled out on that hillside to this day; or until Metro made their morning rounds and either hauled me off to jail or died laughing, whichever came first. That was not the last of my mishaps at that location, although the violence diminished somewhat after the first accident.

One night, I had my pallet made up and my canopy in place. I was on my hands and knees, puttering with my blanket. Suddenly I started tipping over. I did not feel dizzy; I did not feel anything. I just started falling over. Fortunately for me that time, I did not have far to fall. I could not stop myself and went clear to the ground, bumping my head on my cart as I fell. It was a comparatively gentle bump, as it did not leave a lump on my head. I was more surprised than hurt, but I still did not get the message that the hill was bad news for me.

I had been wondering for some time, though, how much longer that community would put up with the mess that the campsite had become. I should have listened to myself before I learned the answer to my question the hard way.

One funny thing did happen while we were camped at that location. Not that the incident itself was so funny, but Eddie's interpretation of it was hilarious. One evening, just as we were getting settled down for the night, a car with a man and a woman drove up the driveway. It parked in front of Eddie's and my camps. The couple sat there for a few moments, then turned around and drove back down the driveway. Eddie made up the following scenario for them.

Hubby, waving his hand in the direction of the makeshift tents as well as the recumbent figures lining the fence, declares to his wife, "See, honey, that is the way those people live."

Wifey gazes obediently at a scene that is obviously unfamiliar to her. She then turns to her husband and says, "You know, dear, I don't think we need that extra bathroom after all."

Satisfied that he had made his point, hubby turns the car around and drives back down the hill. I was weak with laughter for the next half hour and I did not have time to feel lonely, scared, or think, "Oh my God, what am I doing here?" that night.

People wondered why a woman my age, who must have gotten some kind of a pension, lived as I did. I did get a Social Security check, but at the time I earned my maximum income, wages and salaries were not nearly as high as they are now. Therefore, the Social Security accounts did not build up as rapidly as they do today. Although not high by today's standards, federal income taxes still used to be too high on lower income. They were so high that Social Security was the only savings plan I could manage.

Adding all this to the fact that I took my Social Security at age sixty-two, losing twenty-percent of the income I would have received at sixty-five, it was not difficult to understand why my income was not adequate for the higher prices by then. Fifty years prior it would have seemed like a fortune. A little over twelve years ago, at the urging of friends, I applied for Supplemental Security Income (SSI). At that time in Nevada, the monetary amount of SSI was not very high, but the medical benefits were good, and I needed an operation on one eye.

Although my application was approved and I received two or three checks, the clerk who had helped me fill out the SSI application at the Social Security office said at one point, "This is state welfare, you know." The Social Security office had at that time application forms that could be filled out in their office. The completed forms were then forwarded to the SSI office, which was not as conveniently located for me as the Social Security office was.

Until then, I had not given much thought to what Supplemental Security Income was, and the word "welfare" turned me off. I was so proud of my Social Security income because I had earned that.

Shortly after I got on SSI, a fire gutted the Triple

A Hotel, and I was forced to find another place to stay. With the help of the Catholic Community Services Senior Citizen's Employment Office, I obtained a live-in house-keeping job and took myself off SSI.

The people at the SSI office had tried to talk me into deferring this action until they could review my case and determine whether or not I might still have qualified for their program. But I was so smart; I was going to do the job myself. Now, I wished I had listened to them. I wasn't able get it done by myself, and now I am nearly blind in one eye. At the time I resigned from the SSI assistance, I also dropped the food stamp assistance. That agency had allowed me a whopping ten dollars a month in stamps, so resigning from that program worked no great hardship on me.

Now after all these years, I am considering getting back on SSI if I can, and having the operation on my eye. If I make any profits from this book, I hope to be able to repay the state for its help.

That was what my father did. When he was in his late sixties, Dad needed an operation, but he did not have the money for it. The county paid for the operation. As soon as Dad was able to work, he got a job and repaid the county everything he owed. That was the spirit I admired. What Dad did was not easy for him. He worked in a hard-ware store where he had to be on his feet, but he hated having to accept charity.

It was October 14, 1989. We were sitting, stand-ing or lying in the parking lot waiting for the yard to be opened. The sun was about to make its appearance, and there was a chill in the air. The days were still hot, but the nights were getting cooler, just right for comfortable sleeping.

It was getting close to Halloween, and I was

reminded of Halloween a year before. We were waiting for the yard to be opened that day, too. Some of us were discussing the upcoming celebration and kidding each other about going trick-or-treating Halloween eve. Bernie was a nice young man with a somewhat happy-go-lucky attitude toward life. As we told each other our "plans" for the festive evening, Bernie told us his.

"I'm going to cut my hair, shave off my beard, and go trick-or-treating disguised as a normal person," he announced happily.

Bernie and I, too, had gone back to the days at the Triple A Hotel where we were residents and sometimes desk clerks. That morning it suddenly dawned on me that in four more days I would have reached my seventy-seventh birthday. What was a nice old lady like me doing, living out there, and where had the years gone? As fast as they were flying by, I just knew that Father Time must have put quicksand in his hourglass to speed things up a bit. Lordy, it was difficult to think out there. Normally, I had little difficulty in shutting out unwanted noise and concentrating on what I was doing. Yet, that morning, there was a group sitting at a nearby table that seemed to be constitutionally unable to speak in a normal tone of voice. Everything had to be shouted at the top of their lungs. Even for me, so many decibels were hard to handle.

The sun was well up by that time, although it was not so high that the people walking in back of me had created a strobe light effect on my paper. That too was distracting, but if there were no environment there could be no book, so I had no complaints. I had hopes to make it off the street before I finished the book, and to have it end with that happy event. It's beginning to appear as though what I have looks more like a continued story than a proper book with a happy ending; a soap opera perhaps, or The Perils of Pauline.

I wonder how many people are around today who remember actress Pearl White as the continually imperiled Pauline? That dates me like my birth certificate. Pauline, my birth certificate, and I have all been getting along in years. I don't know how Miss White felt about her adventures, but I knew that this not-so-heroic heroine was getting awfully tired of her perilous existence.

As far as I was concerned, Jason and Ulysses and Sylvester Stallone were welcome to life's more hazardous ventures; they had the youth and the stamina for them. I guess Miss White did, too. But as for me, in the unlikely event that I did get out of that mess alive, I was content with admiring the exploits of these intrepid heroes on late-night television. Adventures are much less searing when it is someone else who is having them. The question in my mind then was: would I ever make it safely back to civilization? Or would I meet my doom in the form of a shopping cart suddenly gone berserk?

These were not such farfetched possibilities, as it might seem to the inexperienced. One windy day, I was sitting by my cart, working on some of the word games and puzzles (of which I am an ardent fan) when I heard someone call out, "Mary, your cart!"

I looked up to see my cart, driven by wind, speeding across the yard toward the back fence. This was a distance of probably a quarter of a block, or possibly a little more, from my parking place. I leaped from my chair and sprinted after the errant cart, but it had too good a start on me. I could not catch it. The buggy finally came to a rest against the fence, where it waited for my arrival. The wonder was that it had not run over someone along the way, or that its wheels had not been caught in one of the numerous large cracks in the pavement and overturned.

Chapter 4
Fame Is so Fleeting

St. Vincent's Plaza was once a fair-sized shopping center. Except for the two or three businesses that, I suppose, had long-term leases, the building had been vacant for some time before St. Vincent's acquired the property. They did have their problems with the old structure, and so did some of the cats that first shared the premises with the humans.

The cats had established their quarters in what I imagined was sort of a loft area above the dining room. I was never up there to see it, so I did not know what it looked like. One day, several of the kitchen workers were sitting at one of the dining room tables, working on produce for future meals, when one accident-prone feline fell through the ceiling and landed on the floor near the men. They said the cat was not injured, but I bet it was surprised.

Another adventurous kitty picked the site of its mishap with more care. The ceiling over the hall, which we went through on our way to the dining room, was not as high as is the dining room ceiling. This was where the ceiling tiles gave way with the second cat. The furry acrobat also had the forethought to break its fall by landing on the head of one startled patron waiting in line for his bowl of soup. Neither man nor beast was injured in that accident, either.

Most of the cats were wild, but two of them were pets. I didn't know where Tiger and Calico came from, but they were special. Tiger was a big, tiger-striped tomcat; one of those unusual animals that seemed to be more human than animal, except that it was nicer than many people. One day, during the time I was working in the dining room at St. Vincent's, I met Tiger in one of the halls leading to the dining area. When I stopped to pet the big cat, he stood straight up on his hind legs and pushed his furry head as tightly as he could into my hand.

Another cat, Calico, as her name implies, was a multi-colored female that had her first litter while I worked for St. Vincent's. Even though it was her first experience at motherhood, Calico was a good mother, and the kittens thrived. Tiger was never even suspected of being the father of the little ones because none of them looked like him. But from time to time, Tiger took on the job of kitten sitting for Calico when the busy little mother had other business to take care of. He endured the indignities heaped on him by the disrespectful babies with exemplary patience.

Although he had no children of his own that we knew of, Tiger seemed destined to be the doting uncle type. One had the feeling that if he were human, Tiger would have his pockets loaded with presents for the children when he came to sit with them. Some of the men who stayed at St. Vincent's also took an interest in the little family and made pets of them. They often put the kittens in a box beside them while they were playing cards in the big room in back of the dining room.

Eventually, of course, the Public Health Department insisted that St. Vincent's get rid of all the cats, pets or not. Mr. S., who was the manager of the dining room at that time, took Tiger with him when he quit his job, but not on account of the cats. We were told that homes had been found for the kittens, and Calico was consigned to the guard office upstairs where a bed had been prepared for her. I don't know how they got rid of the wilder cats. Some of them refused to be housebroken, and they were a problem, all right.

For a while we used to see Calico when we went upstairs for our showers, but I hadn't seen her for a long time and did not know what became of her. Even though we knew the Health Department was in the right, we still missed Tiger and Calico and the kittens.

It was one of my blah days and I hadn't even felt like writing. It was Sunday and there were no showers that day, so after lunch I decided to lean my head against my cart and take a nap. I was just dozing off when Greta tapped me on a shoulder and asked me if she could borrow a needle and thread. The prior day, she had insisted on giving me a dollar for the thread she had been using. This day, I would gladly have given the dollar back to her if she would only let me sleep.

There seemed to be something about seeing me sleeping that stimulated my friends to these irresistible bursts of activity. Sometimes they even woke me up to ask me if I was all right. I told them I would be if they would let me get some sleep. Even if I crossed over the Great Divide in my sleep, I would at least be rested for the journey. No amount of logic moved them, however, so I guess I should have felt thankful that someone cared that much about me. I tried.

It had been a dropsy day, too. Practically every thing I touched, I dropped. I don't know that it was so much that I dropped things, as it was that gravity reached up and snatched them out of my hand. That's what it felt like, anyway.

Another day and garbage soup again. That was what one woman I know called the soup she made when she cleaned out her refrigerator. Her husband, whose hobby was gourmet cooking, calls it even less elegantly, "pig slop." He retired to his den in disgust whenever the concoction was brewing. If I ever get to keep house again, the leftovers will go around once as leftovers. Anything left over after that goes into the garbage—no soup.

I once worked in a tearoom in a posh Detroit suburb. The owner made her employees eat the leftover food until it was gone, no matter what its condition was. It was a wonder we did not all die of food poisoning, but as far as I knew, nobody ever did. That might have been one of the experiences that inured me to the later life experience of living on the street and eating anything that was given to me. Even though the tearoom episode occurred over fifty years ago, times were hard then, too, and I had a child to support. A job was a job.

One day two men, obviously of Hispanic descent, stopped to ask me if I had a needle and some thread they could borrow. When the men brought the needle back to me, they not only insisted on paying me more money than the snippet of thread they had used was worth, but a couple of days later they brought me a sack of fresh tomatoes.

I never asked for or expected payment for the thread, or for the loan of needles and scissors. I felt it was something I could do for my companions. Some people were not conscientious about returning the needles and scissors, and from time to time, I lost both. Most people, however, were honest.

Many of the street people earned a small income donating blood plasma to the "stab lab," or the "vampire room," as the blood plasma centers were variously called. Although I do not recall ever having heard of them being given credit for this contribution, I often wonder what the hospitals would do for the plasma they needed if all the homeless people were run out of town. I have heard from several of the donors that Las Vegas is one of the lowest-paying cities for plasma. I bet the hospitals paid plenty for it, and their patients even more.

Gathering aluminum and copper for the metal recycling centers was also a popular way to earn money on the street. From what I've heard, Las Vegas also does not pay as well for these metals as do some other places. But it was coffee and cigarette money sometimes, provided the centers' scale wasn't off, as I heard they sometimes were. Without the metal collectors, I can visualize a community knee deep in empty cans. "They also serve who only stand and wait," or donate plasma or collect cans, however humble they may seem.

Were it not for my not-so-dreary friends, life out there would have been dreary to the point of madness. Some of us did have one rather interesting experience when St. Vincent's was at its old location on south Main Street. One sunny November afternoon, some of us were variously sitting, laying or standing around the yard, when one of our men came through asking for volunteers to do a job that afternoon.

A movie company was filming a picture in Las Vegas. It was the story of a man who comes to Las Vegas, loses his money (not an unusual story), and winds up eating at a soup kitchen. Mr. Ryan O'Neal was the star of the picture. The producers had decided to film the soup kitchen scenes at St. Vincent's and to use actual street people as extras. We would be paid ten dollars for our afternoon's work.

Happy to have the opportunity to earn ten dollars, and thrilled at the prospect of working in a movie with the popular Ryan O'Neal, a number of us volunteered for the job. We were lined up along the inside of the fence as we usually were at mealtime, and were told to behave as we normally did. Obediently, we stood in our usual line, engaged in our usual horseplay, and teased the handsome young man from the kitchen who, in the picture, would open the gate for us at twelve o'clock.

They were getting ready to start production, but the prop man had a problem that day. They had a sign reading "Free Food," which they intended hanging over the "Donations" sign on the side of the building, but their sign was not being very cooperative. No sooner would the men get the sign up and turn to walk away than the recalcitrant sign would fall down. This happened several times, and those prop men were getting awfully red in the face. I suppose they had a schedule to keep, the light was changing, and what I imagined was some very expensive time was being wasted.

We gave them what helpful advice we could think of, together with our sympathy. Finally, because of our efforts or in spite of them, the sign decided to give up its battle for independence and stay in place. It was just about in time to ward off an epidemic of apoplexy among the prop men. Shooting began!

We had been instructed not to look across Main Street, where the camera was situated, so we kept our gaze turned carefully away from that direction. But no one had thought to warn against making too much noise. They had told us to act normal, and normally, we made some noise. Too much noise obviously, because in a few minutes, a man came tearing down the line. With more than a trace of irritation in his voice, he told us we were too noisy. They could hear us clear across the street.

We apologized for our unseemly behavior and after that, we pantomimed our conversations and cut down on our horseplay. I thought we were doing rather well for a bunch of amateurs. After that, our performance must have improved with the change in our modus operandi, because we received no more complaints. In a short time, someone again came down the line, but this time it was not a reprimand. Instead, we were told that there would be a short break while Mr. O'Neal was being made up for his role. We could sit down if we wished, but we were not to change our places in line.

I was wearing a heavy vinyl coat, as the mornings were getting a little chilly, although the afternoons were warm. I did not dare take my coat off, so I literally sweated out the rather long wait while the makeup department labored mightily to make the handsome Mr. O'Neal look as much like the popular conception of a bum as possible. They had overachieved. The next time we saw him, the star had lost his luster. He looked like the bummiest of bums, much worse than most of us did. We would not have dared walk down the street or into a casino looking that seedy.

It was so unlike his usual appearance that we could not help but laugh. Even the star had a sheepish little smile on his face as he rolled his eyes in our direction. The indignities the movie stars will endure for their art! I guess they earned those big salaries, all right.

I said to those standing near me, "Remember folks, there isn't a camera within a mile of us." Until then, I had not realized that there was a repressed director lurking around somewhere in my subconscious, as I was not normally a bossy person. I did not usually have enough confidence in my decisions to tell other people what to do. Whatever the case, Mr. O'Neal said, "For any of us."

I was at the head of the line, and the action seemed to be taking place farther back, so I could not see or hear what was going on. It seemed the rest of the shooting must have gone without a hitch, because soon the star was coming down the line, thanking us for our work and signing autographs for those who requested them. He "God blessed us" as he went out the gate. Ryan O'Neal was one nice man. There was nothing high-hat or put on about him. We loved him.

In the movie, two young women who played the part of the hitchhikers were also very pleasant. They acknowledged with grace the wolf calls from some of the men. I don't know who it was, but I heard someone say, "Be sure these people get their money." We were given our ten dollars and the remains of what appeared to be box or sack lunches. Cigarettes were also distributed.

I later heard that the movie showed in Las Vegas, but I did not see it. One man who did see the picture said that the soup kitchen scenes went by so fast that it was impossible to tell who was in line. I could have taken off my heavy coat. We could have changed places in line and changed the whole line, and the audience would never have known the difference. Fame was so fleeting—ours was, anyway—but we still made ten dollars and got to meet Ryan O'Neal. I would never forget that.

CHAPTER 5
GOD AND MAN CARED ABOUT US

One of the ways the homeless survive is through the kindness of the community. It was Sunday afternoon, and I had just finished eating two bologna sandwiches and drinking a diet cola. I had also put aside a huge muffin for the next day's breakfast. A group calling themselves Friendly Services for the Homeless brought the food to us, as they had every Sunday for several months.

One, or possibly several of the Adventist churches also brought sandwiches and punch to the parking lot early Sunday mornings before the yard opened. A lot of time, work and money went into these projects. They were truly labors of love. The Catholic Franciscan Order of Monks and Nuns worked in conjunction with Homeless Advocacy Project (HAP) and had recently opened a building on the corner of Las Vegas Boulevard North and Owens Street.

It was called Friendship Corner. It had a number of features designed to assist homeless people in coping with their circumstances, or if possible improving them. There was a mail receiving service for those who had no mailing address. A free telephone enabled prospective employers to contact prospective employees and vice versa.

A washer and dryer had been installed for the people's use, and there was space where possessions could be stored free of charge for ten days. AP also published a monthly paper called *HAPpenings. HAPpenings* told of activities by and for the homeless, and published contributions by the homeless: articles, poems, stories, cartoons — anything with potential interest. *HAPpenings* also listed "hot spots," areas where the police were *a little too assiduous* in their attentions to the street people. Shelters, soup kitchens, and social service offices where people can get help were also described in the paper.

One group of people from a Korean church in Las Vegas brought food to the yard one day a week and served it to us. One Christmas, while I was still working in the kitchen at St. Vincent's, the owners of a Las Vegas Chinese restaurant brought fortune cookies to the kitchen workers at St. Vincent's. In each cookie was a two-dollar bill. The Chinese are not only clever people, but also generous.

For the first two winters I was out there, and possibly before that, one man brought donuts and a large urn of hot chicken or beef broth to the parking lot each morning at 6:00 o'clock. The story was that this man was once on the street, and when he became more prosperous, he did not forget what it was like outside. Nowadays though, this work has been taken over largely by church groups or by St. Vincent's. There are so many more people out there than there used to be. It would take a very prosperous person, indeed, to furnish coffee or broth and donuts for all of them.

Several hotel casino resorts provided holiday meals, too. These were really sumptuous traditional holiday feasts, the provider's skimp on nothing. One year at St. Vincent's dining room, we were not only served a great Christmas dinner, but as we entered the dining room, we were handed an envelope containing a ten dollar bill. Rumor had it that a well-known resort mogul furnished both the meal and the money. I didn't know whether or not the rumor was true, but I knew that both the banquet and the money made that Christmas much more enjoyable for a lot of lonely people.

It is difficult to put into words what the shelters and the soup kitchens mean to the homeless. They were like pieces of heaven that offered a welcome temporary shelter from the onslaughts of the elements. They were a break from the loneliness of the great outdoors that was stretched from here to eternity around us. I could not have survived long without them, and neither could a lot of other people. This also goes for the people who brought us food, clothing, and other material things, as well as what was possibly the greatest gift of all—their caring nature, which gave us the assurance that both God and man cared what happened to us.

Intellectuals frequently seemed to be people who had opinions about everything under the sun, whether or not they knew what they were talking about. Although I had some tendency toward intellectuality, I did not know if I could have been called an out-and-out intellectual, but I did know that I was born opinionated. When I was very young, my family tried to teach me the simple, quintessential nursery rhyme, "Mary's Lamb."

This seemed to be easy enough for any halfway intelligent tot to master, but not for this miniature know-it-all. When it came to the lamb's fleece, I balked. Everyone knew there was no such word as "fleece"; the word had to be "face." The adults were trying to make a fool of me. They did not have to try very hard, I suppose, until I was old enough to read the rhyme for myself. Mary's lamb had a white face, whatever the color of its fleece might have been.

It was not difficult to start an argument with an intellectual. All one needed to do was to open one's mouth; the argument followed naturally. One day a couple of the men, Sarge and Emory, were standing near me and talking. Ordinarily, I did not barge in on other people's conversations, but both of these men were friends of mine, and we conversed frequently. So, when Emory said he had read that some psychologist had said that there was absolutely nothing good about television, I could not resist the temptation to join the conversation. It was the word "absolutely" that had gotten to me.

I said there might be a lot of television that was worthless and inane (there always would be as long as people would rather be entertained than enlightened), but then I cited such programs as *60 Minutes, Meet the Press and Face the Nation.* I also mentioned the newscasts, which took us right to the scene of significant world events. A privilege that was heretofore reserved for the participants therein, and a few journalists. I must have scored a point because my opponents fell back on those ubiquitous and mysterious "theys" who seemed to have so much to say about human affairs.

We heard only what "they" wanted us to hear, and saw only what "they" wanted us to see. Naturally, if time or space were considered, we would get an edited version of the news. This was unavoidable, but I was not able to get enough words in even edgewise to make that point. I could not overcome the odds of two to one against me, so I finally threw up my hands in mock despair and told my adversaries that I should have known better than to argue with them.

This provoked a sort of spin-off from the original discussion in which both men denied vehemently that they had been arguing. I didn't know what they were doing, but I was arguing. In an impressive display of self-control, however, we managed to refrain from calling each other stupid, although on their side, the implications were there. At one point I remembered telling them that their arguments were utterly without logic. But we did not actually mention the word "stupid."

I don't think that arguing ever accomplished anything anyway, except to convince the participants therein that all the others are blithering idiots. Before reaching this conclusion, however, I once again allowed myself to be drawn into another heated non-argument with Sarge and Emory. This discussion concerned the necessity for attending school in order to get an education. My opponents contended that one could learn all one needed to know without ever attending school. This might have been true under some circumstances, such as being able to afford years of private tutoring or having a rather narrow view of what one needed to know. Under normal circumstances, however, I still opted for a formal education. I had no doubt that some people would have the determination, the self-discipline and the IQ to educate their selves. Emory and Sarge probably qualified, but I doubted if I would. I had no idea what percentage of the world's human population could accomplish such a feat.

What baffled me about this second go-round was the fact that Sarge and Emory were well-educated, well-read men. Sarge had been a master sergeant in the United States Army, and Emory had studied for the ministry. They were hardly ignoramuses. As in the previous discussion, neither side was able to make a dent in the opinion of the other. We finally gave up the battle as a lost cause. Again, we parted company with our friendship intact; probably because we did not call each other stupid that time either.

I decided then that dyed-in-the-wool arguers do not really expect to convince anybody of anything; they just liked to argue. As for me, I was an education buff. It is one of the big regrets of my life that I did not go to college. Pontiac High was an accredited school, and I had taken its college prep courses so I could get into a university without having to take an entrance exam. My parents were hard hit by the depression of the thirties, and they could not send me to college, which they would have loved to do. Some young people worked their way through college, but I did not have the enterprise necessary to do that.

Occasionally, intellectuals come up with some fascinatingly off-beat ideas. One afternoon, Margaret, one of the yard intellectuals, and I had an interesting if somewhat weird conversation when we lived at the Triple A Hotel. We were lolling around on our bunks one day. The hotel must have been suffering from an infestation of ants, because suddenly Margaret said, "I wonder if the ants are writing books about us?" I took the bait—hook, line and sinker. "Oh, Margaret," I protested, "ants can't write books." "How do you know they can't?" she countered. "If they did, they would be too small to see." That logic stopped me. How did I know that ants couldn't write books just because I had never seen an ant writing a book; nor to my knowledge have I ever read a book written by an ant? But of course, I had never read a book written by an ant. It would have been too small to see, wouldn't it?

Margaret worked as a desk clerk at the Triple A Hotel, and she also worked at some of the owner's other enterprises. Eventually one of the other hotels at which she was employed was sold, and Margaret lost her job in the reorganization of the hotel by its new owners. Now in her sixties and after a series of major operations, it was not easy for her to find a job that would pay enough to support her. Margaret, like Sarge, tended to be a bit of a pessimist. One could start an argument with her just by saying, "Good morning." "What's good about it?" she would snarl. I couldn't begin to snarl as well as Margaret did. "Well," we said, somewhat taken aback, "we're here."

For this, we were likely to get a sneer. But by this time we were beginning to warm up to our job. "It isn't raining," we persisted, unless of course it was raining. In that event, we knew better than to say "good morning" to just about anybody except Hughie. He was determined to remain cheerful no matter what Mother Nature was doing. Margaret just grunted.

Sure that we had her that time, we played our high card. "Metro didn't get us this morning," we announced triumphantly. Margaret was undaunted, not to say adamant. "Wait a while," she advised sourly, "It's still early." At this, we conceded defeat and left our pessimistic friend to enjoy her pessimism in peace. To each his own.

Margaret's mother, who passed away when Margaret was in her teens, must have been a veritable saint. Margaret told me that if her mother could not think of something good to say about a person, she would tell a fib rather than badmouth the person. Margaret lost her father some time before her mother passed away, leaving his wife with five children to bring up.

Margaret also told me that all four of her brothers had been killed in one or another of this country's various wars or peacekeeping activities. No wonder their sister hated war as much as she did.

Margaret's maternal grandfather worked on the construction of some of the great railroad bridges, which spanned the mighty gorges of the Rocky Mountains. One day, some of us who were acquainted with Margaret were discussing the matter of someone of her caliber living on the street. We said that Margaret had missed her calling in life. I thought that she should have been an astrologer; she was very good at astrology. It was she, in fact, who had given me the information about the location of the planets Jupiter and Venus, which gave me the idea of using them as timepieces.

Some of the others, however, said that because of

her love of books, Margaret should have been a librarian. The quiet atmosphere of a library would have suited her temperament well, too. I agreed with them, but I could not resist teasing Margaret a little.

"I'm not so sure that being a librarian would be such a good idea," I said. "Somehow I can just see Margaret standing at a check-out desk and snatching a book out of the hands of a startled patron, as she says sternly, 'You can't take that book out. I haven't read it yet.'"

I don't know whether or not Margaret had forgiven me for that remark, and I didn't have the nerve to mention it to her. After all, one of Margaret's chief complaints in life was that even if she lived another twenty years, she would not have time to read all the books she wanted to read. I knew what she meant.

When the federal government tried to get St. Vincent's to turn the women's dormitory into a shelter for mentally ill women, Margaret quit her job as manager of the dormitory and came out to the yard to live. I had preceded her by a few weeks. The job did not pay anything anyway, although she had been promised the white card of a supervisor and the salary, which went with the honor. She had worked in a mental hospital at one time, however, and she did not want that kind of a job again.

Not all mentally ill people were violent and dangerous, of course, but some were. Many of them were turned loose on the street to fend for themselves as best they could, and they sometimes would threaten other people. Anyone who did not believe that could try sleeping a few feet from such a disturbed person—especially when you're outside in the open, without protection—and see how much sleep you'd get.

"Can you spare something to eat? I have to lose weight. If I lose some weight, I will have more energy. I don't know how to make love. I have to get my brother out here to show me how to make love."

This was the greeting I received from one young woman when I went to a nearby trash can with, of course, some trash. I am not making fun of a mentally ill person; mental illness is no laughing matter. I used the above quotation only as an illustration of the sort of thing that went on much of the time out here. Sometimes it was a stream of profanity shouted at the top of their voice for hours at a time, while the affected person paced the yard from one end to the other.

I overheard a frightening conversation one day while I was working in the kitchen at St. Vincent's. My routine job was in the dishwashing department. There was a window in the wall, between the dishwashing corner and the hall, through which the diners passed when they left the dining room. There was someone stationed in the hall, outside the window, at mealtimes. They would to take the trays and eating utensils from the departing guests while stacking the articles where the dishwasher operator could reach them.

On the day I was referring to, several new men had come to the kitchen to work. One of these men was stationed at the window that afternoon. The job sounded simple enough, but by the time the bowls were taken off the trays and stacked, any leftover food or other trash was dumped into a large garbage can placed in the hall for that purpose. The trays were stacked for the machine operator. The job was quite time consuming. When the diners start leaving in droves, the situation became positively hectic, and the window person was kept jumping for a while.

It took experience to keep things moving, but the new man was not even trying to keep up. Instead, he simply stood at the window for most of the noon period.

He said that women had caused all his problems, and he glared at me. I didn't remember how the rest of us in the dishwashing department got our work done that day, but I remember that it wasn't easy.

The most disturbing event, however, occurred as I was taking off my apron and preparing to leave the kitchen. I didn't know how I managed to be the last one in the kitchen, except for the woman-hating window man and one of the other newcomers, but somehow I did. The men were talking, and I heard the window man say,"Sometime I just feel like killing someone."

"I know," the other man replied, "but you just have to fight it."

I think that at one time or another, most of us have said, "I was so mad at so-and-so today, I could have killed him," but we didn't kill anybody and didn't really want to kill anybody.

My mother's close friend, whom she had known from childhood, had a habit of saying, "Hate 'im, kill 'im dead." Yet, Bertha was so gentle, I doubted that she ever so much as swatted a fly or spanked her children. The very thought of actually killing anyone, or any creature, would have thrown Bertha into total shock.

However, there was something in the tone of their voices and the serious expressions on their faces that told me they were deadly earnest. The "deadly" might have been the definitive word for them. I did not know what the backgrounds of these men were, but numbers of criminals were sent to the soup kitchens and shelters to work off the community service, which was part of their sentences. Heaven only knows what those men might have done to land them at St. Vincent's, although they might not have been criminals at all. We simply did not know where they came from.

Some of us had complained about the men's behavior to D.M., who was the head cook and boss of the kitchen. He told us that we should be more tolerant of people with problems. D.M. was a nice, clean-cut young man, a Vietnam veteran who had served as a cook in the United States Navy. This alone would have prejudiced me in his favor, but because of my age, he was also very good to me. That was the kind of a man he was.

I do not believe, however, that the possible danger of the situation had come home to him. He had not heard the men's conversation and the seriousness of their voices; nor had he seen the equally serious expression on their faces.

Those men were not just kidding around, as some of the rest of the kitchen help was inclined to do. I didn't think that D.M. remembered all those big sharp knives lying around the kitchen, free for the taking. The knives were not kept under lock and key. They were easily available to anyone who wanted them. The thought of a possible threat had occurred to me though, and with good reason.

On two occasions my life had been threatened by disturbed, knife-bearing women. The first encounter left me with a cut on my forehead, just above my eyes, but the second woman was intercepted before she got to me. Then she lived in St. Vincent's yard, as I did, and we were on friendly terms. Thank Heaven!

Neither of those incidents occurred while I was living on the street. The first attack took place while I was working in a private home. I was living at the Triple A Hotel, when the second woman decided that she disliked me enough to kill me. I did not care to try for a third strike in this scary ball game; the third one might be fatal.

I felt sorry for those men. They were obviously

not enjoying their condition, but it was a big relief to me when a day or so later, they disappeared from the kitchen. D.M., of course, had nothing to say about the people who were sent to the kitchen to work. It was his job to utilize them as well as he could. I did not envy him his job.

Working in the kitchen did have its lighter moments, though. One day, when Margaret was working the window, we had another contingent of outsiders assisting us in the dishwashing department. As we stood around waiting for the trays and bowls to start coming back to the kitchen, someone turned to Margaret and said, "Tell them to eat faster, Margaret. I'm beginning to grow moss on my north side."

Another man, whom I suspected of being mentally disturbed because of his generally aberrant behavior, came to me one day when I was sitting beside my little post. He said something about playing cards. Although I had never seen this man doing anything as normal as playing cards, I explained politely that poor vision kept me from playing cards. My unwelcome visitor told me that I lied and called me a fighting name.

As he was too big for me to fight, however, I could only watch him closely as he circled my chair. I wondered if he intended to sneak around and tackle me from behind. After muttering a few more insults, my tormentor finally gave up his little game and wandered aimlessly away, much to my relief. The fact that this man slept in the same camp I did was not exactly soothing to my nerves. One night he stole some money from Greta, who also slept in that camp. I heard that some of the other men stopped him before he did anything else to her. This guy might have been crazy, but he wasn't crazy enough to pick on someone his own size. He seemed to specialize in picking on women or the handicapped. That sounded pretty smart to me—not very nice, but smart.

This wasn't the first time in my life I wished that I was 6'4," weighed 250 lbs., and was all muscle. Whether the pusher was sane or insane, I did not like being pushed around. Though the mentally ill cause problems, they also have real problems. They got robbed, raped, beaten, and murdered, either because they could not take care of themselves, or because they antagonized people by their behavior. These things also happened to people who were not mentally ill and for much of the same reasons, or for no reason. There were a lot of mean people in the world.

A man went into a campsite on the hill, which I had only recently left. He tried to get in bed with some of the women. When they rejected him, he kicked them. He was a stranger, not one of the yard people. He also kicked one of the men, an older man, because the victim refused to give up his blanket when the intruder demanded it. Then the goon told the older man that he was lucky he wasn't dead. To be 6'4" tall and 250 lbs.; there I go again. Wouldn't I have loved to put that jerk in his place!

This particular morning, when we were waiting in the parking lot for the yard to be opened, a tallish, seedy-looking white man suddenly appeared among us. Going to Margaret's cart, he tried to snatch one of her blankets. We thought he was the same person who terrorized the campers on the hill a couple of nights ago.

When Margaret protested his action, he started to curse her and refused to leave. We were not the mild-mannered people on the hill. Some six or seven of us closed in on the man, ready to stop him if he became physically abusive. Perhaps I would have had a chance at this idiot after all. Still refusing to give up, the man said loudly that he just "wanted a blanket to cover his frigging arms."

One of our men called out to the rest of us, "Does anybody have a blanket so he can cover his frigging arms?" No one did. After a few more curses from the man, and more protestations from Margaret that she did not have a blanket to spare, the would-be blanket snatcher finally strolled out of the lot. He was still without a cover for his frigging arms, except for his suit jacket sleeves.

He was a nervy one, but no one needed to steal a blanket around there. At that time of year, when the nights were turning cold, all one needed do was ask for one at St. Vincent's. They usually had extra blankets, which they would give away. During the cold months, people also brought covers to us. A week or so ago, a truckload of pillows and comforters were driven in to the lot and distributed to those who wanted them.

A few nights after this incident, a man came into our camp early in the morning before we were up. He tried to get in bed with one of the women. I didn't see the man, but it sounded as though the same person was wandering around, trying to get himself into a heap of trouble. In this most recent caper, some of the men in the camp drove him off.

So far, he seemed to have picked on older men and on women, but we had some very rough younger men in our camp. If that man got them riled, he would be the one lucky to be alive. I learned from a friend who camped near me that the blanket seeker finally got his blanket. To be more accurate, he got somebody else's blanket.

Risa was awake at the time and saw what happened. She said the intruder was drinking with one of the campers until the intended victim fell asleep. Then the thief snatched his blanket and ran out of the camp. The man who lost his blanket was still asleep when I left that morning, so I did not know his reaction to his loss, but I bet it was a chilly one.

Alcohol does not act as an anti-freeze in the human

system, as it does in the radiator of one's car. Every winter in Las Vegas, someone who had been drinking fell asleep outdoors and froze to death.

At least one of these cases would attract media attention. This resulted in an outcry in the community, which was highly critical of the shelters for letting someone die in the street. However, some people would rather sleep outdoors than to put up with the rules and restrictions of the shelters. That was their choice, not the shelters.'

CHAPTER 6
I WOULD RATHER BE WITTY THAN ITTY

I was again camping on the hill across from Foremaster Lane, although since the day of the "mass arrests," I had never felt completely at ease on that hill. My camp was farther up the hill in an old cemetery. I did not believe that I was unduly superstitious, but there was something about the thought of walking on or sleeping on somebody's grave that made me feel very uncomfortable.

I made my camp about ten feet from a darling leprechaun of a man, a good friend of mine whom I shall call Paddy, and two or three of the other older men I knew. I was awakened one night by strange sounds coming from Paddy's direction. Paddy sometimes had nightmares and made odd noises, so at first I merely turned over and tried to get back to sleep. Then I heard Glen say, "He doesn't have any money. He's broke."

At that, all thought of sleep vanished. I sat up and looked around. I saw several of our men standing around Paddy, and another man, unknown to me, standing at his head. I did not see the second stranger, but Paddy told me the next morning that he had been awakened by the hands of one of the visitors around his neck. The other man went through his pockets.

This was the second such incident perpetrated against Paddy while I was sleeping there, and Paddy told me there had been others. It infuriated me that Paddy was being so mistreated. I wanted us to get clubs and teach those hoodlums a lesson they would not want to have repeated. But those men were a peaceful bunch, and they would not go along with me. They were probably right. We might have gotten into something we could not have handled, although the man I saw did not look like a member of any of the neighborhood gangs I had seen. He was too old, for one thing.

I think they were just individual bad guys. They might not have been so brave if they were faced with five or six people who were armed with clubs and determined to defend themselves; but I will never know.

Not being able to do anything to help Paddy really galled me. Sometimes when a treat was brought into the yard for us—ice cream or sandwiches or whatever—Paddy managed to get two of whatever it was. He would bring one to me. There was always a rush for these goodies. I did not have a chance against stronger, younger and faster people, but Paddy did. He could push and shove and grab with the best of them, and that was what he did; but now there was nothing I could do for him.

The man I saw picking on my friend that night in camp took a long look at me on his way down the hill. I had to wonder if he figured I probably got a check at the same time Paddy did. Since there was nothing I could do for my friends, and that hill was beginning to look uncomfortably dangerous to me, I found another campsite closer to St. Vincent's, and once again moved off the hill.

One day, during my first year out there, I was sitting in my chair and working one of my word puzzles. A voice behind me said, "Mary, will you have sex with me?"

At my age, I could think only that one of my friends was having a little fun with me. However, I could not think of any of them who would speak to me in such a manner, even as a joke. In an effort to be a good sport about the whole thing, I turned to make some laughing rejoinder. Sure enough, I did not recognize the young man standing in back of my chair. He wasn't laughing, or even smiling.

"We could go into the restroom," the man continued. I knew then that he was not kidding. Furious, I leaped from my chair. In a tone loud and clear—especially loud—I told him what he could do with his sex. The man said nothing during this tirade. He just stood and looked at me with a strangely detached expression, as though he was wondering what all the fuss was about. He might have been on a drug of some kind; he looked so detached. That thought did not occur to me until some time later.

Although the men at the nearby pinochle table had not heard the young man's question, they knew there had to have been something said or done to upset me that much. Emory looked threateningly at the still unmoved man as he said, "How would you like to have about fifteen men on you?"

At about the same time, another man from a few carts down the line came over and started herding my tormentor toward the yard gate. Before he left, still showing no emotion and offering no resistance to my rescuer, the guy gave me one final look and said, "You're a woman." Since this tidbit of information did not come as news to me, I did not consider it to be an insult. I ignored it and sat back down in my chair.

Curious, Emory asked me what the man had said that made me so angry. When I told him, he said that he did not blame me. But one of the other men saw the matter in a somewhat different light. With just a hint of admiration in his voice, he said, "Well, at least you know you still have 'It.'"

I hadn't thought of the experience in quite that way, and did not feel particularly thrilled at the idea. At my age, I think I would rather be witty than "Itty." Wit is much less wearing than "It."

For months after that incident, I could not make even the mildest complaint about feeling my age without some wise guy reminding me that things couldn't be all that bad. "After all, you've still got 'It,' you know." Hughie in particular delighted in twitting me about my "It." I hadn't heard the term for over a year though, nor had I received another proposition, so I guess I had finally lived down my reputation as an "It" girl.

One interesting and slightly amazing incident occurred in the parking lot one morning. It was still quite early, and only a few of us were in the lot. I was sitting on my overturned bucket, waiting for the yard to be opened, and feeling unusually despondent. "Here I am," I thought, "living outdoors. I need to know more about it." Would you believe at that very moment, one of the men walked up to me and handed me a copy of the *Outdoor Living* magazine.

The exquisite timing of William's kindly gesture amazed me so much that I involuntarily laughed. Judging by his expression, William must have thought I was deriding the idea and wouldn't be interested in a magazine of that kind. I wanted to explain the reason for my laughter, but the shyness (which had plagued me for most of my life) kept me from saying anything except "thank you." This reaction was somewhat surprising to me because I thought I had gotten over much of my backwardness.

A reporter who visited the yard a few times to gather material for a series of articles on the homeless told me that I had found my strength on the street. I think she was right. It my new self-confidence arose from my circumstances. One would not think them conducive to the development of self-confidence, but the result was total acceptance of me by the other street people. They never treated me as an outsider. I was always one of them. They laughed at my witticisms and treated me like a queen. They made me feel so smart and important.

I was so changed that when I had a chance to talk to William a few years after the magazine incident, I was able to remind him of it and explain my laughter. Judging by his reaction to my little speech, William had not thought anything of it after all, although he did say that he didn't think the *Outdoor Living* magazine would be much help out here.

I had to agree with him. This was probably not the type of outdoor living that the publishers of the magazine had in mind. Even so, I did find several articles of interest in that issue. I still remember them, and they helped pass the time very pleasantly that morning. I used to be a fairly outdoorsy person—hiking, swimming, fishing, rock hounding, etc.—but after enduring so much outdoorsiness, I don't think that the great outdoors will ever again have the same appeal for me that it used to have.

I thought I overcompensated for my shyness a bit, and sometimes I spoke up—then later wished I had just gone on with my crocheting. At the time I came out to the yard, I had begun to realize that the creeping threat of old age, which had been dogging my footsteps for some time, had accelerated it's pace to a fast gallop and was rapidly overtaking me. I suddenly became very conscious of my age and was fighting my impending doom, tooth and toenail.

When anyone but my biological descendents called me "mom," "grandma" or "granny" when I was at work, it made me feel a thousand years old, more or less.

One day two young men, who had not been in the yard very long, were standing by my chair and talking. One of the men wanted to say something to me, but he did not know my name.

"I call her Mom," said the other man. Before I knew what I was going to do, I turned and said, more sharply than intended, "My name is Mary."

The men were obviously taken aback by this unexpected rebuff, and I had a problem trying to explain it, so I didn't. How could I tell those nice men that they made me feel old enough to be Methuselah's mother? That would have sounded like a reprimand for something they had not intended to do. Hopefully, they will read this book one day and accept my humble apology for my unwarranted rudeness. I hope try to understand my explanation for it, which was more than I did.

When I was young, I did not think that older people were ugly. I liked older people and had loving relationships with them. So why did I feel so differently about myself? It baffled me. I had to know that old age would catch up with me if I lived long enough, but nobody told me it would feel like that. If there was one thing in life that should not surprise us, it's old age. It seldom strikes us overnight; we have plenty of time to think about its eventual advent.

I don't believe that most people really enjoy the thought of looking or feeling old. In fact, I read that most people do not feel old; they just feel like themselves. I believe that out on the street, the older people often act as parental or grandparental figures for some of the younger persons who are far away from their families. That thought did not occur to me for some time, but it was somewhat comforting when it did.

There was also a touching conversation in the coffee and donut line one day, which was of some help in my adjustment to my age. I was lamenting the fact that I was just a useless old woman, but a young man standing near me said, "Oh, I don't know about that. Sometimes when

I'm feeling upset, I look over at you sitting there with your crocheting and I calm right down." That man had lost one of his arms in the military service, I believe he said. I was especially happy to have been of some service to him to whatever small degree.

I was sitting in my usual spot when another young man—a young black man this time—walked up to me and said something about his mother. I don't remember now what it was, but he knelt beside my chair and asked me if I loved him. When I assured him that I did love him, he got up and walked away smiling. The human touch was as important out there as it was any place else, perhaps even more so.

CHAPTER 7
LAUGHTER WAS A FACTOR

I really must have been wrapped up in writing this book. One night, when Archie got to his campsite, he found a beautiful, high-back, wood and upholstered chair. The upholstery was gold colored, and the chair looked like a throne. Someone must have brought it into the camp during the day and left it there. Since no one had claimed the chair by morning, Archie appropriated it and brought it to the yard.

When I went over to get a look at his new treasure, I found Archie sitting on his golden throne, his face beaming with pleasure. I wanted to say, "Hail Archie I," (using his real name, of course) "Emperor of Las Vegas!" But for the life of me, I could not think of anything but Archie. He did not know about my book or his part in it, as far as I knew. As I did not feel like going into the matter at that moment, I stood there like an idiot trying to think of a name that I knew as well as I knew my own.

Finally, after what seemed like an hour, although it was probably just a matter of seconds, the name popped into my mind and I completed my obeisance. Archie was delighted. I don't think he had noticed the lapse. As far as I was concerned, Archie was a king, with or without a throne. I was very fond of him.

We had been following the news of the earthquake in San Francisco on a radio that belonged to one of the men. What could one say about such a disaster? It had always seemed to me to be such a shame that any place as beautiful as California should have such problems. Not that any place should have them, of course. It's just that when I first came West in 1936, I settled in Long Beach and immediately fell in love with California.

The booming surf of the sparkly Pacific had the snow-capped mountains in the background. I had never before seen an ocean or a very large mountain. The palm trees, the majestic Seventh Fleet lined up in all its glory on Battleship Row in the harbor; all this enchanted me. I guess when we're young, everything is new and enchanting.

Then there was the climate. Oakland County in Michigan, where I grew up, was a county adorned with lovely blue jewels of lakes. Its gently rolling hills were green with grass and woodlots in the summer. In the spring, its fruit orchards would glow with the pink and white blossoms of apple, peach, cherry, plum and pear trees. Fall brought a mosaic of colors: scarlet, yellow, bronze and russet, mingled with the lingering green of summer. It, too, was part of America's great beauty, but the cold, damp winters had always been bad for my health. Perhaps I would feel better in the milder climate of California.

I thought that California must be where the Garden of Eden had been located, although I did not remember that the Biblical account of the garden mentioned a nearby ocean. Anyway, it just seemed to me that such a paradise should last forever, undisturbed by anything as upsetting and destructive as earthquakes.

My Uncle Alf, however, did not agree with me one hundred percent on the charms of California, especially when it came to the palm trees. Uncle Alf was brought up among the graceful elms; the spreading chestnut, oak, and maple trees; and the shimmering draperies of the weeping willows, which abound in Michigan. When he saw for the first time one of the tall, slender palm trees with the tuft of fronds on top, but otherwise devoid of foliage, my uncle could not believe his eyes. He stared at the monstrosity for a moment, and then he exclaimed disgustedly, "That is the poorest excuse for a tree that I have ever seen."

I think that remained his opinion of California and its palm trees for the rest of his life. He and Aunt Minnie were getting on in years, and I think that their three daughters, all of whom lived in the Los Angeles area, wanted their aging parents near them.

One woman I know had an eerie, if possibly life-saving experience in connection with the earthquake. The day before the disaster, Janice and one of her daughters left their home in northern California to drive to San Francisco on a business trip. After their business was taken care of, they planned on driving home through the redwoods, which they had never seen. When they got to Santa Rosa, however, the car started slipping out of gear. Not wanting to take a chance on getting stranded somewhere on the highway, Janice decided to go back home and make the trip to San Francisco another time.

After that, she had no more problems with the car. The next day, of course, the earthquake struck, and some people did not believe in guardian angels or anyone.

One morning I asked Margaret if she would mind being in my book. "Not if you tell the truth," she replied. "Just don't say anything that cannot be backed up by a shot of sodium pentothal."

Margaret was a devout believer in the power of sodium pentothal to worm the truth out of people. In fact, she believed it should be used in criminal cases to get accused persons to tell the truth. Since I did not intend to say anything about Margaret that could not be backed up by a shot of truth drug, unless she herself had given me false information, Margaret was in.

It was getting close to the time of year when we were wondering if we would be sleeping in St. Vincent's shelter again that winter. When we did sleep there, the tables and benches in the dining room were folded up and put out of the way after the 6:30 p.m. coffee and donut break. Mats were put down on the floor. A smaller, carpeted room adjacent to the main dining room was reserved for women and children.

I did not believe that the mats were more than two feet wide and they were placed only a few inches apart— very few. This much togetherness could make a problem out of what was ordinarily the comparatively simple act of turning over at night. Under the circumstances, turning over without bumping your neighbors was almost impossible. This provoked occasional bitter arguments between the bumpers and the bumpees, who objected to being startled out of their sleep by those sudden close encounters. Snorers were not very popular, either.

Last year the supervisors of Project Sleep at St. Vincent's decided to do something special for the women and children, so they reopened the women's dormitory. This move gave us our own quarters completely away from the men. The floors were carpeted, and there was a television lounge and an inside restroom nearby. No more going outside to porto-toilet in the middle of the night. It could have been a nice little setup for us, but as usual, there were those who could not appreciate what they had, even when it was all they had.

There were arguments every night, and even some really vicious fist and kicking fights. I had never seen anything like it among women. Occasionally, one of the women brought booze into the dormitory with her, although alcohol in the shelter was strictly forbidden. The weather was very cold that winter, and I think management was at somewhat of a loss as to how to handle the situation. They were reluctant to put a woman out in the cold, especially in the middle of the night, and especially in that rough neighborhood.

As stated before, any time a transient freezes to death in Las Vegas, the shelters have a lot of explaining to do, even though the deceased might have chosen not to go to a shelter or not to obey the shelter rules. On the other hand, the way we heard it was that a member of the Las Vegas City Commission had threatened to visit St. Vincent's shelter unexpectedly at night to check for booze on the premises. If any were found, the shelter would be closed. That winter I thought that the management at St. Vincent's just hung in there and prayed for an early spring so they could close the shelter.

Some of the women were pregnant, or thought they were. Sometimes the condition was obvious, and sometimes it wasn't. A few of the prospective mommies seemed to be in continual danger of miscarrying. The paramedics were called to the shelter so many times, for what turned out to be false alarms, that they got tired of the situation. One medic threatened to bring a mat and stay at the shelter, but another was sterner and told the shelter monitors not to call them again unless there really was an emergency; otherwise, they were not coming out. It was remarkable how rapidly the ladies' health improved after that ultimatum was issued.

Monday, December 21, 1989, I was sitting in my chair crocheting when someone came up behind me. She threw their arms around me and gave me a big hug. It was Allie. She and Archie had separated. Even though I knew she was hurt by the breakup of her marriage, she was as bubbly and bouncy as ever. Since the separation, she had been shuttling back and forth between Las Vegas and Florida. The last time she was back East, she bought a van, something she had wanted to do for several years.

One year she bought a motorcycle. It was not quite the vehicle of her dreams, but transportation. She started to ride the cycle to Las Vegas, but when she got about halfway across Florida, she decided there were more comfortable ways to travel. She sold the motorcycle and rode the rest of the way on a bus. It was definitely more comfortable than a motorcycle; not as exciting, but more comfortable.

I told her I was writing a book and asked her if she would mind being in it. I could never write for the tabloids. I did not really enjoy invading people's privacy. I didn't want to be sued for something indiscreet I might have said, either.

Allie said she did not mind and I could say anything I wanted to about her. She did not mention sodium pentothal, but I didn't intend to say anything that bad about Allie, either.

I let Allie read what I had written to see what she thought about it. She was particularly struck by the name I had chosen for her. She said her mother's name was Allie. Neither she nor I could remember her ever having mentioned her mother's name to me, but perhaps she did and it lingered in my subconscious. It was certainly not a conscious memory. With her usual bubbling enthusiasm, Allie said, as she handed the manuscript back to me, "Oh, Mary, it will sell millions!" I hoped that this optimistic assessment of my labors was not influenced entirely by the twin facts that she wanted to encourage me and that she was featured in the book.

Allie plays pinochle and was one of Sarge's favorite players, even though she could not resist crowing over the men when she beat them. Sarge would not take that from anyone else, but Allie's laughter was so contagious that I think it lightened up Sarge's day. Besides, Allie was a good card player, and she always gave the men a run for their money when she played cards with them.

Friendly banter was a way of life in the yard. One day, Archie and a tall, nice young man whom I shall call Jeremy, were engaged in this type of badinage. In response to some insult from Jeremy, 5'4½ Archie looked up at 6'4" Jeremy and said firmly, "Only a tree is that tall." The "tree" merely smiled tolerantly, but I nearly fell off my chair laughing. Jeremy was a gentle giant.

Some of the pinochle players, however, take their card playing with almost deadly seriousness, and their banter was anything but friendly. Since I decided to omit really nasty language from this book, I will not go into the lurid details of some of their conversations and of the names they called each other. Suffice to say, two hundred years ago, they would have provoked duels to the death between the participants. For our group, it was not unusual for some irate player to slam his cards down on the table and depart the scene in high dudgeon, to say nothing of high gear.

One day one of the men turned to me and said, "When are you going to play cards with us, Mary?" I explained that impaired vision precluded my playing cards. What I did not say was that even if my vision were 80/80, I would not play cards with those barracudas. I used to play pinochle and liked the game almost as much as Sarge did, but my game was never of the championship quality, which Sarge demanded of his players. Although, I won a lot of card games in my time, including pinochle games, with or without a partner.

The first time Sarge called me stupid—which he would not do in a debate, but pinochle is something else—I too would slam my cards down and leave the table in a rage. I valued my friendship with Sarge too much to take a chance on our becoming bitter enemies over a card game. To dedicated pinochle players like Sarge and me, the game took on more the dimensions of a cause than it did a recreation. I still would not like being called stupid.

To further illustrate just how seriously Sarge took his pinochle playing, I heard him say that one day, when he had made some kind of a booboo—misplaying triple aces or a double run or something (Sarge's group played with double decks), he was so embarrassed that he left the table and didn't go back for a week. I had also heard him say that he and his wife had played in card tournaments for money. That would tend to make one take his card playing seriously, all right. Sarge's opinion of people tended to depend largely on their prowess as a pinochle player; the better the player, the better the person. I guess that was as good a standard as any.

Ferdie was a gentle soul and a fair-to-middlin' pinochle player, who sometimes filled in at the pinochle table when one of the regulars could not make it. One day Ferdie was having a particularly rough run of luck, or non-luck, and after several games, he was low man on the pinochle totem pole. The top man in that day's play could not resist doing a little gloating by saying how lonely it was at the top.

Ferdie looked up from another less-than-adequate hand to observe plaintively, "It's lonely at the bottom, too." Ferdie had a naturally plaintive voice anyway, and that made his remark all the more poignant.

I don't know whether it was that we were more easily amused than the average person, or whether we just didn't have much else to do. But, we seemed to do a lot of laughing out there; especially when one considered our circumstances. Or perhaps laughing was one factor that helped us hang onto such sanity as we did have.

But funny little things did happen quite frequently, in fact. One of them occurred at night, when we were waiting to get in line for our 6:30 p.m. coffee and donut break.

Vergil, a dignified middle-aged man, started walking toward the yard restroom. Thinking that he had lost track of the time and was headed for the dining room, one of the other men called out helpfully, "It isn't 6:30 yet!" Vergil turned with his usual stateliness and asked seriously, "Does that mean I can't go to the restroom?"

Since it did not, he turned back and proceeded to his destination without further interruption. The rest of us cracked up. In addition to the other contributions he made to our lives, Hughie was determined to furnish us with some of life's lighter moments. One day, before we knew each other very well, Hughie came over to me and said, "Hello, I'm your next door neighbor. I came over to see if I could borrow a cup of money."

This so amused me that when my next check came, I put some money into a casino change cup and presented it to him. It was his turn to be amused, but since pulling his little joke, Hughie had bought a jar of instant coffee and some cigarettes for me. I hadn't made my check stretch for the whole month, so I owed him. The borrowed cup of money became a standing joke with us.

Hughie was the first person I heard say that when his ship came in, he was at the airport. I have heard others make the joke since then, but they didn't have Hughie's delivery. He could break me up just by saying, "Good morning." I am the same age his father and mother would have been if they were still on earth, and Hughie took a somewhat protective attitude toward me. Age did have its advantages.

One of his standard replies, whenever he was asked to do the slightest thing, was, "How much money are we talking?" One day he came to the table where some of us were sitting and chatting. As he walked up to us he said, "Well, I have my washing done and dried; now I'm looking for someone to do my ironing. How about you, Mary?"

"How much money are we talking, Hughie?" I asked.

He was so amused at having one of his favorite phrases thrown back at him that it, too, became one of our ongoing jokes. Judging by some things he had said, I think that Hughie and his mother did a great deal of kidding each other, and I imagine Hughie missed that after she passed away.

He and I still had our carts under the arcade when a couple of men who camped near us decided to reorganize their carts. They were trying to decide where to put things, and I heard one of them say, "Put the bleach on the table."

"No," the other man replied. "If I do, Hughie will drink it."

"No he won't," I contradicted. "That would turn him white, and Hughie doesn't want to be white."

The two men did not seem to think that remark was very funny, but Hughie said, "That's right; I'm black all the way through." Despite the one man's implication that Hughie would drink anything, Hughie never had been a boozer, although another of his little jokes was that one of these nights he and I would go out and hang one on. We would have to take a designated walker with us to help us get down the Main Street hill without disaster, as the first sip would probably turn our legs to rubber—all four of them. That at least was my experience when I used to drink some, a long time ago.

CHAPTER 8
IF LOVE WERE THE COIN OF THE REALM

Thomas was a black man probably about my age, and he was a veteran of World War II. He still suffered miserably from a hip injury received in that war. Three operations had not relieved the condition. Thomas worried about the women on the street, especially when the weather turned cold. On the first really chilly night, he did not think that I looked warm enough covered by my one blanket, so he brought an extra sleeping bag he had and put it over me. He also put more covers on another woman who did not look sufficiently covered.

All I could say about some of the people out there was that if love were the coin of the realm, some of the people would be living in mansions. I suppose the vice versa situation would be true.

Eventually, Thomas got his own place. He used to visit the yard once in a while, but the last time I saw him he was in a wheelchair and on oxygen. I hadn't seen or heard about him in a long time, and I did not know whether he was still on earth or not. People would come and go out there, but our friendship lived on. Perhaps some place, some time, we would meet again. I certainly hope so.

I don't follow a pattern in crocheting, preferring to make up my own designs, mostly because I found following instructions to be a tedious job. Tearing out and starting over could be pretty tedious too, and I did a lot of that. As a result of this trial and error, I occasionally came up with some weird looking creations.

The first year, I decided to make mittens for the

people in the yard. I had never made mittens before, but I knew what a mitten looked like, and that was my starting point. One of my early efforts resulted in a pair of mittens with outsized thumbs—really outsized! I had intended them for L., but he nearly fell down laughing when he saw them.

"I'm going to find a hitchhiker," he chortled, "and tell him, have I got a mitten for you!"

With perseverance, however, I did better and finally got a pair of mittens that did fit L. On my first attempt, I even managed to make mittens to fit Jeremy's long, slim hands, so I improved with practice. Seeing me busily crocheting away day after day, one of my neighbors nicknamed me "Madam La Farge." I guess the principle was the same even though the craft was slightly different. I thought it was funny, anyway.

Several men stopped by to tell me that they had learned to crochet while they were in prison. One man made such beautiful afghans that he was able to sell them while he was in prison, and when he got out as well. Other men were taught the craft by a woman close to them—a grandmother, a sister, an aunt or a girlfriend. I hadn't realized that there were so many men who enjoyed that activity, but there were.

For a while I had a good supply of cigarette lighters at very little cost. One of the men had good luck finding lighters, and he brought them to me to trade for a few cigarettes. This might not have seemed like much of a price for lighters, but I never knew how much fluid was left in the torches when I got them, unless they were the see-through type, which they usually were not.

Sometimes someone would donate a lighter to Nat. He was walking along the street one day when a small boy threw a lighter out a car window, hitting Nat on the head with it. Not one to pass up an opportunity to turn a mishap into a profit, Nat retrieved the lighter and brought it to me for one of our usual deals.

A fight broke out near me one day, and as I usually did in such cases, I leaped from my chair and ducked behind my cart. Some man, no one from the yard, had too much drink and came to the yard looking for trouble. He found some. It was a white man he had picked on, but some of the younger black men hurried over and told the belligerent intruder to take his fight away from that old lady. Then one of the men turned to me and said with a smile, "You don't have to move, Mary. You have too many guardians that will take care of you." I appreciated that assurance, even if it did surprise me.

One morning, one of the men asked me for a cigarette. I told him I was completely out. Then I started wondering if "completely out" was any more out than just plain "out." When we say that we are completely out of smokes, though, we mean we really are out and are not just telling a fib. We do not want to share our last two cigarettes with someone.

It looked like rain, and that was probably what we would get. Rain was forecast for a couple of days, but mercifully the night was clear. I left my sleeping bag wrapped in a plastic bag. That way if my blanket got wet the night before, I would have something dry for the next night. If it rained very hard, we might be allowed into the large conference room at St. Vincent's; then I could write.

If it was both windy and rainy. I could not write outdoors, as both hands were occupied with holding my large piece of plastic over me like a tent. We were truly a plastic society. Furniture stores discarded the large plastic envelopes in which mattresses were shipped, and we found all sorts of uses for those envelopes. We used them as covers for our carts to keep out the rain, as tents for ourselves, and as mats, which we spread on the ground under our bedrolls to keep them clean and dry.

We made all sorts of adjustments for the weather out there. In the summertime, for instance, the fierce desert heat melted the mucilage on postage stamps and envelopes, so I'd buy stamped envelopes at the post office.

Some of the people thought of their spot as being their home, not their camp. Sarge said that he was not camping out; this was his home. He defended his spot as though it was really a home, too. That sometimes involved a certain amount of violence. One misguided soul, who moved into Sarge's territory one morning after the yard was cleared, pulled a knife on Sarge when he tried to reclaim his "home." The tough old sergeant ran the man off anyway, without the help of any of his neighbors. Sarge had been a master sergeant in the United States Army and was a seasoned combat veteran. Even in his sixties, he was no pushover.

For years, Margaret had been trying to get me to take notes on our adventures and misadventures on Skid Row, with the intention of one day writing a book about them. Until then, however, I had pooh-poohed the idea. I did not feel too proud of my circumstances, for one thing. In fact, I found them downright embarrassing. Also, I could not believe that anyone could possibly find them interesting.

One day, I heard Sarge say the social worker was trying to find an affordable apartment for him. The worker asked him how people survived out there, especially the older people. This made me wonder if Margaret might have been right after all. Since the social worker was curious about this matter, perhaps enough other people would be curious about it, too. It would make writing a book on the subject worthwhile. I decided to give it a try. If it did nothing else, it would help pass the time, although at that point I did not realize how much time would pass. If I wasn't old when I started the book, I would be positively ancient by the time I had finished it.

I know at least one man who wasn't too thrilled at living like a tramp, either. One night, when we were sleeping in the field in back of the grocery store, someone had apparently gone to sleep with a lighted cigarette and had set his mattress on fire. However it happened, we were just getting settled down for the night when one of the men came running down the path. He asked people if they had any water. I offered what little water I had in my water jar. Then someone remembered that there was an outside water tap at the nearby car wash. I got out my bucket and offered that.

I don't know what happened to the others or how I got roped into the job. I guess I just followed my bucket. But the next thing I knew, Rob and I were the only people left who were working on the fire. Although Rob did not even sleep in the field—he had a camp closer to town— he had obtained a bucket from somewhere. Together we toiled through the night from the tap to the stubbornly burning mattress. The distance was probably close to a city block or half a block, anyway.

In a misguided attempt to sound a comforting note, I said on about the umpteenth trip, "Look at it this way, Rob. Ten years from now, you'll look back on this night and laugh."

"No I won't," was Rob's emphatic denial. I think I knew how he felt. I didn't believe I would ever laugh about it either. A few minutes later, when I was scooping up dirt and dumping it into holes that I had cut in the mattress cover, Rob said, "You must have been some woman when you were young."

I'm still trying to take that as a compliment. Rob was a little taller than me, and I am 5'5½, but one of his favorite complaints was that he was just an inch short of being able to screw that light bulb into the socket. He had two main ambitions in life. One was to be tall enough to put that light bulb in place, and the other was to reach the height of mediocrity. I don't know what one had to do with the other, but Rob always lumped them together in his speech. He, like Sarge and so many others, was a veteran of the United States armed services.

I haven't seen Rob for several years, so I do not know whether he ever attained his goals, but I know one goal we did not attain. Despite our hours of hard work that night, and even after running around until we could see no more hot spots in the mattress, when I got up the next morning, some of the men were once again working on that fire. Don't those things ever go out? We probably did not call the fire department because we thought we could handle one little mattress fire ourselves. The grocery store was not threatened, and I suppose we were afraid that the field would be closed to us if we called in the firefighters.

CHAPTER 9
A LOUSY LOUSE

Perhaps this book might more aptly have been titled, "Too Little—Too Late." Most of my life I had been a chronic "also-ran," so I suppose it was only fitting that I should spend my golden years living on the street. When I was in junior high school, my main ambition in life was to get on the National Honor Roll. Excellence did not come easily to me, and I never was a straight A student. Math could always trip me up, if nothing else did, but I worked very hard to achieve my goal.

I could have made it with points to spare, had I not met my nemesis in the person of one of my classmates, whom I shall call "Wimpy." No scholar himself, Wimpy was determined that I would not enjoy the fruits of my labors. Unfortunately for me, Wimpy and I shared several classes. In every one of them, he heckled me so bad that I could not recite. Every time I was called on to recite, he mocked, derided, and talked me down. I might have been able to out yell him had I tried, but my sense of decorum, a quality utterly lacking in Wimpy, would not allow me to create shouting matches in our classes.

I handled the situation in the only way I could think of. I refused to recite in class. My written work was up to its usual standard, and my teachers knew perfectly well that I knew my lessons. Much to Wimpy's swaggering delight, however, they kept me after school to warn me that they could not grade me on recitations I refused to make. Since they said nothing about quelling Wimpy, I saw no sense in letting myself in for more of his tormenting, so I maintained my silence and did not get my A's in those subjects.

I still missed the honor roll by not more than a point. So near, and yet so far. I was devastated and wanted desperately to quit the public school system and go to the Catholic school. St. Frederick's was where scholastic excellence was encouraged and the sisters kept strict control of their classrooms. My family did not belong to the Catholic Church, however, and if I recalled correctly, non-Catholic students were required to pay tuition in order to attend Catholic schools.

Although Dad was a hard worker and Mother was a whiz at managing money, my parents did all they could to keep three children in public school. They couldn't afford the tuition. That was the closest I ever came to making the prestigious honor roll. Seventy years later, I still felt the disappointment.

Except in written composition, my career in high school was not exactly distinguished, but I could not blame that on Wimpy. I do not know what became of him after junior high; I don't remember seeing him in high school. Maybe he was still floundering in ninth grade, but he was finally out of my life. I never learned why he picked on me as he did. Up until the harassment started, I didn't recall that we ever had any trouble. In fact, I didn't remember noticing him at all.

Maybe he was merely envious of someone who was a better student. There were a number of better scholars than I was at Eastern Junior, and they did not have to work as hard as I did, but Wimpy did not torment them. I guess this will forever remain one of life's unsolved mysteries. I have come to the conclusion that Wimpy lost more by his behavior than I did. I still had the love of learning, which enriched my life, but I doubted my tormentor ever knew that blessing. He wasn't the type. I could almost find it in my heart to feel sorry for him; not quite, but almost.

While in junior high, I twice made it to the finals in the annual city-wide spelling bee. In the first competition, I went down ignominiously about half way through the contest, but in my second attempt I did somewhat better. All the contestants, except one other girl and I, had met this Waterloo on one word or another. Virginia, my opponent, came from a family of outstanding scholars. All her sisters had been either valedictorian or salutatorians of their respective graduating classes. Virginia, too, was well on her way to attaining one of those distinctions.

She also had nerves of steel, and nothing flustered her. I, on the other hand, was born a nervous wreck, and everything flustered me. Word after word, the contest dragged on, and with each word the tension mounted. Inevitably, I suppose, the strain began to tell on me. I felt as though at any moment I would fly to pieces, like confetti. Finally, I drew the word, "occurrence." I probably knew how to spell "occurrence" as well as I knew how to spell any of the other words given to me. Unfortunately my treacherous nerves played one of their nasty little tricks on me and I left out one of the r's. Virginia's nerves did not play tricks on her, and she won the contest. Again, I was an "also-ran."

At that time, Pontiac, Michigan, had only one senior high school. The graduates of the east side's Eastern Junior High and the graduates of the posh west side Webster Junior High met and mingled. Virginia lived on the west side of town and probably went to Webster. I lived on the east side of Pontiac and attended Eastern. Virginia wasn't snooty, though. In spite of her scholastic accomplishments and her family's social status, she was a rather quiet, unpretentious girl. One could not help but like her.

I think it was obvious from my description of her that Virginia was hardly the rowdy type. But on the last day of school, before graduation, it was our solemn little classmate who gave us the surprise of our high school career. On that momentous day, a group of us were standing near one of the stairways leading from the second floor to the first floor. Suddenly our usually sedate classmate mounted the stairway banister and rode it all the way down. Such an act might have been expected from me, tomboy that I had always been, but Virginia?

In answer to our startled expressions and exclamations, Virginia explained quite simply that she had always wanted to ride a banister. On that day, she just decided to do it. Maybe she felt that it could be her last fling at childhood, and it was a little late to expel her from school for unseemly behavior. I haven't been able to attend any of my class reunions, and I did not know what happened to any of my old classmates. If Virginia was still on earth, I wondered if she remembered her gleeful ride down that railing nearly sixty-five years ago. I will never forget it.

My failure in the spelling bees was not the last of my scholastic setbacks. I don't know if they still do this, but when I was in high school, the state of Michigan held annual statewide scholastic competitions. High schools throughout the state held contests to choose the best students. The winners in these local runoffs went to the finals held in the lovely little town of Mt. Pleasant, Michigan. I don't remember whether I was in my junior year or my senior year when I won the right to go to Mt. Pleasant to compete in Written Composition as Pontiac High's entrant.

Between the time the high school competitions ended and the day we were to go to Mt. Pleasant, my English teacher kept me busy writing essays. I wrote on every subject she could think of that might possibly be used as the theme for our compositions. After what seemed like a million words or so, the day finally came when we were to board the bus, which would take us to Mt. Pleasant and our latest challenge.

At that time, there was a teacher's college in Mt. Pleasant. That was where the competitions would be held. After we were shown the rooms we would sleep in that night, the various contests began. I have forgotten most of the details of our stay in the little college town, but I still remember how thrilled I was to find myself sitting at a desk in a classroom that was usually occupied by honest-to-goodness college students. This was a *college* classroom—not junior high, not high school, but college. It was a whole new dimension in education. I almost felt like taking my shoes off, as though I was on holy ground. Would I ever become one of the elite, I wondered?

There wasn't much time for daydreaming, however, so I forced myself back to earth. I had paper positioned on the desktop and a pen at the ready. I waited with tense expectations for the subject of our essays to be revealed to me. At last it came: "My Favorite Poem." Miss Lighterness hadn't thought of that one, and if I had a favorite poem, I couldn't think of it at that moment. By the time we were in high school, we must have been familiar with dozens of poems, maybe even hundreds. Yet the only one that came to my frantically searching mind was a charming little number I had read only about two weeks earlier. As I recall, this poem was titled, "To a Louse."

Where was Hiawatha? What had happened to Evangeline? And the village Blacksmith, he had been one of my favorite characters since junior high. Where was he in my hour of need? Even Mary's education-seeking little lamb would have been an improvement over a louse, but the lamb, too, had abandoned me. Time, in its headlong flight through eternity, was rapidly passing me by, and it was clearly the louse or nothing.

I don't think that "nothing" even occurred to me, so I did the best I could with Burns's creepy little playmate and turned in my paper, although not without some trepidation. The trepidation was well founded. When the names of the winners were announced later that day, my name was not among them. I was not even in third place. Despite my feeling that the insect would not do much for me, seeing my worst fears confirmed was a bitter blow. This was undoubtedly the most prestigious scholastic event in which I had ever been engaged, and possibly the most prestigious event in which I ever would be engaged, and the best I could come up with was a lousy louse.

To make the situation even more traumatic, written compositions were one of the four events, if not the only event, in which Pontiac High did not place that year. I was devastated. I was also immature and selfish. We stayed in Mt. Pleasant that night, and no one within earshot of me got much sleep. I bawled and boohooed most of the night. I had let my school down, I had let my teachers down, and I was a disgrace to my father and mother. I was a disgrace to them that night, all right. It was purely a self-pitying, emotional orgy. I had never gotten along well with the teacher who was our chaperone on that trip. If memory serves me right, she was the English teacher who gave me such a bad time about my commas. There were too many of them, or too few of them, or they were in the wrong places.

Finally, in near despair, she told me that in writing I should insert a comma wherever I would drop my voice if I were speaking. I must have dropped my voice in some odd places, because after that she said that I seemed to put my commas in any old place. I could not please that woman. After that night at Mt. Pleasant, however, I felt so sorry for Miss Day that I could never again dislike her. She hadn't gotten any more sleep than the rest of us had. She must have felt the same way about me, because after that trip, the brief encounters that we had were quite cordial. To this day, though, I felt self-conscious about my commas.

A few days after we got home from our Mt. Pleasant trip, a list of the standings of all the contestants had been received in the principal's office and was posted on the bulletin board. Eager to see how the louse and I had done, I hurried down to the office. I had placed fourth in written composition; not too bad considering how populous the state of Michigan was, but still not what I had hoped for.

There was a notation from the judges explaining the standing they had given me. Because of the utter incredibility of the topic I had chosen, they had jumped to the entirely erroneous conclusion that I was satirizing their competitions, and that made them angry. Yeah, right! After all the weeks of practice Miss Lighterness put me through, and the bother and expense my parents had gone to in order to send me to Mt. Pleasant, I was making fun of the contests. The note went on to say that my essay was so good, however, that they could not give me less than fourth place. I could have cried all over again. My big chance to bring honor to my school, my teacher, my parents, and myself, and with the help of a panel of paranoid judges, I goofed it.

As I left the office, Miss Lighterness and a group of students were standing in the hall watching me. I don't recall anybody saying anything, but it was quite clear that they were expecting some kind of an explanation of the fiasco in Mt. Pleasant. I don't know whether or not the teacher believed my story. It sounded fishy (even to me), and I knew it was the truth, but to my dying day, I will never forget the expression of utter bewilderment on her face as she listened to me.

I did win another writing honor in high school, although I did not get quite all the honors that usually accompanied such an achievement. One year, the United States government sponsored an essay contest for school children to celebrate Flag Day. Participation in the contest was not mandatory, and I don't remember why I chose to enter it. I guess I just liked to compete. Those of us who chose to enter this competition were given a copy of the flag manual to study. Later we would be given a list of questions about the flag and would also be required to write an essay about Old Glory.

I must have memorized that manual. I remember working hard enough at it, because I answered all the one hundred questions correctly. Again, some judge must have doubted my ability. When I got my paper back, one question was marked as being incorrectly answered. I knew my answer was correct, and a check of the manual proved that this was true. What did contest judges have against me?

Although I was not able to get the judge's error corrected, I won the contest anyway. I was given the bronze flag medal and got to recite my essay before an assemblage of teachers and students in the school auditorium. The honor that was denied me for this accomplishment was getting my picture and a brief description of my achievement in the Pontiac Daily Press, the local newspaper. I don't know whose responsibility it was to get that information to the newspaper, but nobody did. My parents would have been so proud, and mother would have had an item for her scrapbook. It would have helped make up for the years they had so patiently endured my blundering approach to life's little challenges. Just as excellence had not come easily to me, neither, obviously, did recognition.

The flag contest was the beginning of my love affair with the American flag. I still think it is the most beautiful flag in the world. I cannot hold back the tears of emotion whenever I see our country's banner waving in the breeze. If only the politicians could live up to the beauty and the meaning of Old Glory! If only I could live up to the beauty and the meaning of Old Glory! America would be better as a nation, and I would be better as a person if this were true.

CHAPTER 10
I WAS NOT MADE FOR GREATNESS

In junior high, I was a regular contributor to the school paper, *The Arrow*. I attributed this largely to the fact that my closest friend was an editor on the paper, and *The Arrow* would print anything I wrote. In fact, Ethel and I wrote most of our graduating class's edition of the paper. Ethel, however, did not go on to high school with me; she quit school after the ninth grade and went to work at Woolworth's for nine dollars a week. How I envied her. I wanted to follow in her footsteps, but Mother and Dad would not hear of it. Mother was determined that at least one Truax was going to graduate from high school, and I was to be that one. She and Dad made many sacrifices to attain that goal, or to see to it that I attained it. High school was somewhat different than junior high. I wasn't very good at putting myself forward. Without Ethel to encourage my literary efforts, I performed my stint on *The Tomahawk,* our school paper, as a typist and typed other people's articles.

I was a fast typist, but not an accurate one. It took more years of practice before my accuracy caught up with my speed. Eventually the electric typewriter was born, and the electric typewriter was a whole new ballgame. The touch was very different than the touch on the old manual machines. The keys were a different size and shape than those on the old machines, and the keyboard was slanted differently. It was back to square one for me.

Just as I had longed to make the National Honor Roll in junior high school, so I yearned to get a school letter in high school. Again, I worked very hard to realize my dream. I suppose it follows that the year I was one of the stars of the girls' volleyball team, Pontiac High was not awarding letters for excellence in volleyball. Basketball, yes, but I was a disaster on the basketball court. I was more help to the opposition than I was to my own team. As a guard, anybody could get anything past me, and as a forward, I couldn't have gotten the ball through the hoop without a ladder to stand on, if then. In volleyball, I could stand still and be a hero for part of the game, anyway. Today volleyball is an Olympic sport; how times change.

With volleyball out of the question, the only recourse left to me was success in the track and field events if I wanted to win the coveted letter. I was a fair-to-middlin' runner and jumper. I was not Olympic material, but good enough, I hoped, to get me the letter. I recall that I did pretty well until it came to the rope-climbing event. This event entailed shimmying up a rope, as its name implies. I have no idea how long the rope was, but one end of it was fastened to one of the girders, which held up the gymnasium roof. The rest of the rope dangled far enough toward the floor for us to get a firm grip on it with hands and feet. That, at least, was the theory. Once having attained this grip, we were expected to push and pull ourselves up the rope far enough to touch the girder with a hand.

I don't remember how many times we were given to attain our goal—three, I think. On the last try, I was still about twelve inches from being able to touch the girder, and there I hung. Try as I would, I could not force my suddenly lead-heavy body to move one more inch. So, I missed getting the elusive letter by about twelve inches. By this time, the readers may have reached the same conclusion I had come to. I was not made for greatness; near greatness, yes, but not out-and-out greatness.

I don't suppose being a worrywart did anything to improve my chances of amounting to something. I remember vividly, when I was two-years old, one beautiful Sunday afternoon. My parents and I, and a cousin of Dad's and his family, went to a country club. It was situated on the shore of one of the lovely lakes for which Oakland County is noted. Soon after we arrived at the lake, Dad decided to treat Mother and me to a boat ride. He procured a small rowboat for that purpose.

Any normal two-year-old should have been thrilled at the prospect of going for a boat ride. Any *normal* two-year-old probably would have been, but not this one. None of us were heavyweights. I couldn't believe that the rowboat sank as far into the water as it did. I distinctly remember looking over the side of the boat. Terrified and convinced that with the lightest splash of the oars or anything else — perhaps the backwash from a speeding fish — the water would come rushing into the boat. Surely it would sink and probably drown all three of us.

I did not know how, at that age, I knew as much about the perils of boating. We did not live near a lake, but for an inexperienced two-year-old, I had an active imagination–an over-active imagination was more like it. Anyway, I started to howl. I howled so loudly and so persistently that my well-intentioned father finally gave up the boat ride and rowed us back to shore.

My parents must have fervently wished that they had gone fishing instead on the day they conceived that little pest. If one didn't like a fish, one could always throw it back; not so with a pesky child. This was one of the most powerful arguments I could think of for abstinence. I didn't know where my parents found the courage to have two more children. Life had dealt them such a poor hand on their first try, but they did have another girl and a boy.

My brother and sister, put together, were not as much of a nuisance as I was by myself.

Another occasion for such wishful thinking occurred when I was about five-years old. At five-years of age, I wasn't anymore optimistic about life than I had been at age two. Dad was working on a housing project in Kentucky when a stage version of the well-known and popular comic strip, Maggie and Jiggs, came to Pontiac. Mother wanted to see it.

Obviously forgetting that incident on the lake, Mother made the mistake of taking me to the play with her. After all, what could possibly go wrong at a stage play of Maggie and Jiggs? With my usual ingenuity, I thought of something. We had good seats for the performance. They were in the center section, well down toward the stage. One of the chief props for the play was Maggie's beloved teacart, her status symbol. As I sat in my seat and watched that teacart being pushed toward the front of the stage, I had a sudden terrifying vision. What if someone accidentally gave it too hard a push and sent it flying into the orchestra pit, possibly as far back as we were? It would create havoc and mayhem as it went.

Again I started to howl. I howled so long and so loudly that my mother finally had to take me from the theater. I don't think she ever got to see the rest of the play, nor do I know if she ever found out what set me off that time. No wonder she disinherited me before she passed away at the age of eighty-eight. That was probably the most satisfying thing she had ever done in her entire life. By that time, she had put up with me far longer than even the most devoted of mothers should have been required to do.

Dad, however, loved me to the end of his eighty-four years. I don't know how he did it, especially after

I hooked his thumb with a fishhook in an incident on another lake. In one of his typical understatements, Dad once told mother that I was flighty. To say the least, Dad, to say the least.

Dad had a noble Roman nose, and an equally noble head covered with curly black hair, which even Caesar might envy, except for his eyes of varying colors I did not look like Dad. My head tended to be small and pointed— not like mother's either. I suppose this rather limited space did not leave much room for the cranial convolutions. They are what scientists say hold the gray matter of the brain, the material with which we do our thinking. I suppose that was as good an explanation as any for my behavior. I could blame it all on an inadequate brain capacity. That did sound better than just plain stupid.

On my way to the store one morning, I noticed work was being done on what looked like a nightclub on Las Vegas Boulevard, but there was an "Open" sign on the front of the building. It reminded me of the year the new Lady Luck Hotel and Casino was built. Up to that time, there had been no hotel. There was only a casino, and it was literally falling apart. Every time it rained, the roof was in danger of collapsing. Then one day the new building was started.

The old structure was not torn down to make room for the new casino—not all at once, anyway. In an absolute marvel of constructional ingenuity, the new building was simply erected around the old one. I did not visit the site every day, so I couldn't swear to that. But as far as I knew, the doors of the old casino did not close for as much as one day throughout the whole construction period. The twenty-one dealers went on dealing, and the slot machines went on clinking and clanking. Day by day, the new building grew and the old building shrank.

Finally, there was nothing left of the old casino but the battered little restrooms, huddled forlornly in the midst of the new splendor as though they were hoping that no one would notice their shabbiness. Then they, too, were gone, and the new Lady Luck was complete. It was like watching a caterpillar turn into a butterfly before one's very eyes.

The Lady Luck always had been different than the other casinos. One cold, rainy night, I was out of work and temporarily on the street. That time, too, several other women, in the same fix as me, had taken refuge inside one of the entrances to the casino. When the cocktail waitress came through the casino with a tray of hot canapés for the players, she would give some of the goodies to us, even though she knew we were not playing. I will never forget the young lady's kindness, or the management that allowed it. We would have been run out of any other casino in Nevada, and probably anywhere else.

Strange things happen in Las Vegas, both inside and outside the gambling casinos. I answered the telephone one day when I was working as a desk clerk at a downtown motel. I gave the name of the motel as usual. Somewhat to my surprise, the voice at the other end of the line asked, "What was the name of Lindbergh's plane?" "The Spirit of St. Louis," I answered. The caller thanked me and hung up. For weeks I was puzzled over why anyone would call a motel to find out the name of Lindbergh's plane. Then one day, I heard what sounded like a clue to the answer to the puzzle. I learned that the telephone number of the Las Vegas City Library, which at that time was located in downtown Las Vegas, and the telephone number of the motel where I worked differed by only one digit.

It did not take a Sherlock Holmes to deduce that someone had mis-dialed the library number and had then asked me. That was probably one of the few questions in that whole library of books that I could answer without having to look it up. (Trivia is not one of my strong suits.) That little story is a good illustration of the fact that we hear what we expect to hear. That lady probably expected to hear something like, "City Library," and did not notice that what she had reached was a motel.

Las Vegas also had to be the home of one of the dumbest robbers in all of robbing history. A few years ago, a man successfully held up a downtown bank. He was then captured a short time later sitting on a curb near the victimized bank, gleefully counting his loot.

Dedicated gamblers are not too flappable, either. A would-be bad guy with a gun went to the Horseshoe Casino one day with the intention of robbing it. Security did not dare fire their guns at the man, lest they hit innocent bystanders, so for a few minutes the situation was at a stalemate. Finally the not-so-tough guy gave up on the Horseshoe and crossed the street to the Golden Nugget Casino.

The guards at the Nugget had the same problem as the guards at the Horseshoe, and the intruder made his way to the card room without interference. At first the card players ignored the situation. Then there was a certain amount of hubbub that finally interfered with their concentration. When this happened, several of the players calmly laid down their cards, rose from their chairs and subdued the gunman. Then, after turning him over to security, they just as calmly went back to their game.

Times are changing, though. Since the former paragraphs were written, "tough guys" who were not just fooling around and the incidents of bank robberies have grown to alarming proportions. A number of Las Vegas casinos have been robbed. Day by day this world seems to get less and less funny. Where, I wonder, will it end? Somewhere short of total destruction, I hope.

Some people are not spoiled by sudden wealth. A few years ago, a man in Reno hit a giant jackpot, $1,500,000. For several years, this lucky man had gone to a casino each morning to eat their forty-nine cent breakfast and put a few dollars in a slot machine. On that morning, a machine finally hit the big one for him. He went to the restaurant and had his usual inexpensive breakfast. I don't know whether it was that he, too, was the unflappable type, or whether he was just plain stunned by the sudden acquisition of all that wealth. Whatever the case, he did not forget those less fortunate than himself. He made a generous donation to help the needy.

Not all slot machines are as generous as the machine in the preceding paragraph, and some of them have downright nasty dispositions, as well. Say, for instance, that you were playing a four-spot on a Keno machine and your numbers were four, fourteen, twenty-four, and thirty-four. Not only would this ill-natured type of machine come up with the numbers five, fifteen, twenty-five and thirty-five, but it would growl at you as it did so. This was ugly.

Other machines were more tactful than the growlers, and they would wish you "Good Luck" as you were feeding them. You didn't let them fool you, though. They were just pretending to be your friend so you would give them your money. I was playing one of those hypocrites one day. It was a huge progressive penny machine, one of fourteen machines connected to the same giant jackpot, which was $76,000 at that time.

Despite its cheerful "Good Luck" message, the machine was not paying anything but an occasional cherry. Even though it was only pennies, pennies can go fast when they are being played five at a time. In frustration and exasperation, I turned to the man playing next to me and said, "It's a wonder someone hasn't shot one of these machines by now."

My neighbor told me that one man, also frustrated and exasperated, did hit one of the machines with his hand hard enough to break the glass. Then he hurried out of the casino before the security guard could catch him. A couple of years or so later, I was again playing the penny slots when I heard a crash. Once again, a man had broken the glass of a machine, presumably by hitting it. I did not see what had happened, and he too left before the guard could be called. It was probably the same man who had been involved in the previous incident. He took his slot playing seriously, even if it was only pennies.

Some things are different in Nevada than they are any place else. In Nevada, for instance, diamonds are not always a girl's best friend; not if what she needs to complete a royal flush is a heart, a club, or a spade.

While I am on the subject of gaming, I cannot emphasize too strongly the importance of keeping a close watch on purses or wallets while you are playing. Once, I was playing at a small casino where I usually played. A woman near me was playing several machines at a time, running happily from one to the other. The fun and games ended abruptly for this lady when she discovered that her purse, which she had left sitting between two of the machines, was gone. She said something about having left a man watching the bag. If so, it must have been like letting the fox watch the henhouse, because the man had also disappeared.

Ladies, unless you fall down dead and cannot help it, *never* set your purse down for any reason. If you are standing up with your bag hanging from your arm or shoulder, hold it close to your side and watch that someone doesn't cut the strap and get it. Better still; hold it in front of you.

If you are sitting down, keep the bag in your lap and hang on to it. Purse-snatchers are incredibly fast. They can grab your purse and be out the door before you can even get a description of them or yell for a guard. Don't assume that you can be quicker than a potential thief, because unless you are an Olympic athlete, you probably will not be.

When you go to the restroom, do not set your purse on the floor unless you hold it firmly between your feet. Don't just set it on the floor where someone can reach under the door with a hand or a cane and drag the purse away.

If you hang your purse on the coat hook on the door, hang it on the lower part of the hook. Also place a garment of some kind over it. It takes a fairly tall person to reach over the top of the door and snatch a purse off the hook, but it can be done. Now that you have been warned, you are among the wary and can save your purse.

Since writing the above paragraphs, I inadvertently proved how easy it is to snatch a purse from a toilet booth. At the Shade Tree Women's Shelter one evening, I went into one of the booths without noticing that the neighboring booth was occupied. I put my purse and tote bag on the floor and turned around to sit down. As I sat down, I noticed that a purse about the size and color of mine was lying on the floor in the next booth.

Not looking closely enough and thinking that my bag had tipped over into the adjacent booth, I picked up the purse. To my utter consternation, I realized my mistake when the occupant of the stall emitted a yell of protest. I was so embarrassed that if I had had any place else to go that night, I would have taken my red face out of the Shade Tree, possibly forever.

Fortunately for me, the woman believed my almost hysterical assurances that I had not intended to steal her purse. She graciously refrained from reporting me to the monitor on duty that night. I could not have gotten away with the purse at the Shade Tree, but in a crowded casino, I could probably have disappeared before the woman could have gotten help. It's a traumatic experience to find yourself suddenly stranded in a strange city without money, ID, or credit cards. This is especially true in a tough city like Las Vegas, where the lack of those personal articles can land one in jail real fast.

In spite of all this sage advice on watching one's money, I myself fell for one of the oldest tricks in the book. I was playing one of my favorite machines when a young man sat down at a machine next to me. He told me I had some money on the floor. The crowd at the casino, where I played regularly, was usually friendly. When someone told me I had money on the floor, I usually did. Someone frequently picked up the change for me, so I was not on guard against debauchery at that time.

When I straightened up and turned back to my machine, I saw that the young man was gone. So were some wrapped coinsthat had been in the tray. Fortunately, it was only pennies that were involved in the theft. Not much money was lost, but I felt like an idiot. I've told my embarrassing story only as a warning to other people to watch the money in the tray of their machine.

Another common way of stealing in the casinos is to reach between the -machines from the other side and grab any rolled coins, a bucket of coins, or a purse that might be sitting there. Don't set *anything more valuable than your free casino drink* between the machines.

Men, too, need to be wary when they are in any crowded place. I heard of one young man who took extraordinary measures to protect his wallet. He lost it anyway. To begin with, he wore a tight-fitting pair of trousers so the wallet would fit snugly into one of the hip pockets. For further insurance, he also fastened the wallet to his belt with a chain.

This would seem to have been precaution enough against any thief, but not quite. As he was walking through a casino, he was pushed into a passing cocktail waitress. In an instinctive move to keep the young lady from falling, the man threw out his arms to catch her. In a moment or so, he discovered that while he was being so gallant, someone cut the chain and got his wallet.

There was a question in my mind as to how this robbery could have been performed. It seems to me that the prospective thief had been following the man around. He was hoping that the intended victim would eventually get close enough to one of the waitresses for the ploy to work. Or, the thief and the waitress were in collusion with each other. If the thief had been acting alone, why couldn't any woman have served as the bumpee? Just another mystery added to what seemed to be a growing list of unsolved mysteries. If this kept up, one day I would be able to start my own unsolved mystery television program, although my unsolved mysteries are not as dramatic as Mr. Robert Stack's, thank goodness!

CHAPTER 11
WINDING UP ON THE STREET

One of the men who slept outdoors found a black widow spider in bed with him when he woke up. The spider had not bitten him, and he put it in a jar and brought it to the yard. Although one man I knew said that he had been bitten by one of the creatures, except to their luckless mates, the black widows are not always as fierce as they are thought to be.

A cousin of mine who lived in North Hollywood, California, once found a nest of the spiders in an upholstered chair in her living room. Not one to come easily unglued, Mid reasoned that if the spiders had not bitten anyone up to that time, they probably never would, so she left them undisturbed. I did not know how long humans and spiders shared their quarters, but sure enough, I never heard that the arachnids bit anyone. Even so, whenever I visited Mid, I carefully avoided the spider chair. There was no sense in taking a chance on the spiders not liking me.

I had to go along with Mid, though. I remembered the old story in Roman mythology, to the effect that it was the goddess Minerva, who taught the art of spinning to a young humanity. For that reason, the old Romans held the spider sacred to the helpful goddess. To this day, I cannot bear to kill a spider. Black widows were not the only members of the wild kingdom running rampant in the homeless camps in the area. There were the other kinds of spiders and some really vicious ants, whose bites have sent more than one camper to a hospital for treatment.

Scorpions have also been seen, but I hadn't heard of them stinging anyone. A mild-mannered, non-poisonous-type of snake had also been seen from time to time, but snakes didn't have to be poisonous to send me scurrying from their vicinity.

Due to an alleged rape in the yard, a number of us were required to move our carts from under the arcade roof and out into the compound, where they would not impede security's view of the arcade area. I say "alleged" rape because according to Hughie, who witnessed most of the incident, the young woman had been seen flagging down cars on Main Street. When a car stopped for her, she got in and rode away. In a few minutes, she was back at her stand. It looked as though she was spending a busy evening working as a prostitute.

Later in the evening, she was found in the parking lot, dressed only in her scanties and suffering an epileptic seizure. The man who found her wrapped a blanket around her and carried her into the yard, where the paramedics were called. The story she told at the hospital was that she had been gang raped, probably because she did not want to admit what she had really been doing that night.

Her statement made the men in the yard look bad, and they had only helped the woman. She later recanted her story, but St. Vincent's did not relent in their stance. I remained in my new spot, subject alike to the vagaries of the weather and the onslaught of the pigeons.

For a long time, I was furious at this turn of events. But now I feel only compassion for the unfortunate young woman who caused my displacement. Regardless of my resentment, there wasn't much I could do about the situation except to tie my umbrella to my cart and use it as a canopy against both the sun and the pigeons. When it rained, I fastened my big plastic to one side of my cart and huddled under the "tent" until the rain stopped.

As to the pigeons, the management at St. Vincent's had asked the yard people not to feed the pigeons in the yard because of the mess they made. However, some of the people disregarded the request. So we had a large flock of the nuisances flying in our faces, quite literally, and flapping dirt and feathers onto our persons and our possessions. That is to say nothing of the even messier indignities that they occasionally dropped on us.

Every so often, some of those nasty birds got what was coming to them. Some of the men were laughing at a mite of a sparrow, which had darted down into the midst of a group of pigeons quarreling over a morsel of bread on the ground. Without arguing at all, the sparrow had snatched up the bread and flown straight up in the air with it before the pigeons knew what had happened.

Another pigeon got its comeuppance when St. Vincent's was at its old location on south Main Street. That yard was much smaller than is the present yard, and it was crisscrossed by power lines. Some patio-type tables with attached benches and umbrellas, probably donated by some caring soul, were placed around the yard. Some of these tables wound up under the power lines. Due to the high winds, which had left the heavy umbrellas flopping dangerously above our heads, they had been removed from the tables.

That ensured that an umbrella would not bean us, but it did not protect us from a possible blitz of a pigeon roosting on one of the wires over our heads. That was precisely what happened to one man when several of us were sitting at one of the tables chatting one day. Incensed alike at the injury to his jacket and the insult to his dignity, Jonas picked up one of the hard-as-a-rock dinner rolls, which we had received for lunch that day, and knocked that surprised bird right off it's perch. You can bet Jonas didn't feed the pigeons. A special planet should be created for pigeon lovers, where they could wallow in the mess to their hearts' content.

At about 2:30 a.m., the police coming into camp awakened us. They were looking for a specific person, or so they said. One of the officers was cute. On chilly nights such as that one, we'd wrap up tightly in our blankets and sleeping bags like a bunch of giant caterpillars in their cocoons. When Risa saw that it was the police entering the camp, she pulled her blanket completely over her head and laid as quietly as she could, hoping that she would not be noticed.

One of the officers did find her. He gently pulled the blanket off her face, just far enough to ascertain that she was not the person they were looking for; then he carefully returned the blanket to its original position. Not everyone hated us—not even the police.

One of my neighbors got out of jail and was telling us about her experience. She said that one woman had been sent from the Stewart and Mojave street detention center to the City Hall jail because of her unwelcome attentions toward the other women. The matron would not tolerate that kind of behavior and insisted that the woman leave her jail. Marjorie's comment on this incident was that it was the first time she had heard of anyone being eighty-sixed from jail. Me, too.

A yard woman was hit by a car and was taken to a hospital for observation. We were, of course, concerned about her, so I asked her husband how she was doing. According to him, she had been knocked down in the accident but was not seriously injured, just angered. So angered, in fact, that she picked up her purse and began to beat so hard on one of the car windows that she broke the glass. This frightened the driver of the car. He thought Jo was crazy and called the police.

I don't know how the man expected her to feel. Jo's husband did not say who was at fault in the accident, but being knocked down by a car would be an upsetting experience in more ways than one.

Many people, thousands of them, were on the street because their jobs had been eliminated. This was due to either our rapidly expanding technclogy, or because the work they did was now being sent overseas. There it could be done more cheaply; not only possibly, but probably by forced labor—even child labor under wretched work conditions. These facts were hardly a secret. One of Mike Raddig's duties as the director of Friendship Corner was to help people find work, temporary or otherwise.

Mike told me that the employers of day laborers liked to get these displaced men back whenever they could because the men were such good workers. Most of these employers were quite ethical, but there were some who would take unfair advantage of the desperate needs of the unemployed and homeless for money. They'd come to the yard to recruit workers for a day's work, but when the work was finished, the men were not paid as agreed; or they might be paid with checks, which were worthless or hard to cash.

Not all of these jobs were on or near a bus line, even if the men did have bus fare. If the employer did not provide transportation back to town, which had probably been promised to the men in order to induce them to take the job, they had to make their way back to whatever place they called home as best they could. They usually worked all day at hard labor and had missed whatever meals the soup kitchens had to offer. These were some of the reasons why many of the men would not take this type of work unless they knew the person doing the hiring. I had heard so many of these stories I could cry.

L. was a job-displaced person who had worked as an engineer in the construction of nuclear power plants. Then the government started thinking in terms of nuclear fusion instead of nuclear fission. L. was not prepared for that change, and suddenly he was out of work. Nowadays he takes any kind of work he can get just to survive. Eventually, he joined the job program at St. Vincent's and got to live inside. I think that L. had all of the living on the street that he ever wanted.

He once told me that I was the person he would most rather be stranded with on a raft. It was probably because I knew the difference between nuclear fusion and nuclear fission, and he could talk to me. That would be an important consideration if one were stranded on a raft in the middle of the ocean with only one other person for company.

A woman from Connecticut was temporarily stranded in Las Vegas and stayed at the yard for a while. One day Janie and I were discussing the employment situation in the United States. She told me that there was plenty of work where she came from, but that many of the jobs consisted of going *begging* because there was not enough housing that the workers could afford. All across the country we hear about low-cost housing being replaced by high-rise and high-priced condominiums, or even parking garages or lots. That was what happened to much of the low-cost housing in downtown Las Vegas. As related throughout this book, I had re-met many people on the street with whom I had originally become acquainted at the Triple A Hotel.

I do not remember where I read it, but somewhere I read that Aristotle once said something to the effect that

when the middle class is destroyed and the poor prolif-
erate, the nation will fall. It sounded as though the sage
was speaking directly to this country, didn't it? Maybe
we should listen to him. I cannot bear to think of what
would happen to this world if America, even with all her
mistakes, should fall.

Other people wound up on the street because some
type of tragedy—other than economic—had befallen
them, and they had not been able to pull themselves
together. I met several men whose wives were killed by
drunk drivers. That was the way Sarge lost his wife of
forty some years. They married when they were in their
teens. According to Sarge, they were very compatible,
and her sudden death nearly killed him, too.

For a while a young police officer worked as a
security guard at St. Vincent's. His wife of seven years
suffered the same tragic fate as Sarge's wife. Her grieving
husband had been sent to work at St. Vincent's as part of
the therapy designed to help him recover from the shock
of her loss. I never saw the young man again, but I hoped
with all my heart that the therapy worked for him.

Another man, who worked at St. Vincent's as a
cook for quite a while, also lost his wife of many years in
one of those tragic accidents. Losing a loved one through
illness was difficult enough, but in most although not all
cases of illness, there had been at least some little time to
prepare for the possibility of death. But sudden, violent,
unexpected death had to be total shock.

Although he did not say that alcohol consumption
had anything to do with his tragedy, one man who stopped
in the yard for a few days on his way farther north had suffered a terrible experience. He was a truck driver who was
driving a truckload of flammable material to the western
part of the United States when the load exploded. The

driver was badly injured. But to make one nearly unbearable situation almost indescribably worse, the man's wife and two children were killed in an automobile accident when they were driving west to be with their husband and father.

When I first went out on the street and we were sleeping outdoors, I used my bucket as a toilet at night. I would wrap a coat or a blanket around myself so no one could see what I was doing. The ploy must have worked, as I discovered one night when I was sitting on my little toilet. One of the men came into my camp and invited me to a nearby casino for a cup of coffee. I refused the invitation, politely and with what dignity I could muster under the circumstances, but the man persisted. Finally, in desperation I blurted out, "Look, mister, I'm trying to go to the toilet. Would you please be a gentlemen and leave?"

The man must have been a gentleman—an embarrassed gentleman—because he left precipitately. I lucked out that night. My visitor could have been something less than a gentleman, and I could have wound up with my head bashed in or my throat cut. These things happened in the homeless camps just as they did elsewhere. The lifestyles of some of the rich and famous also include brutal murders. What I wonder is, what is the excuse of those who have all the good things this world can offer? Maybe they are just bored.

One cold, star-spangled evening during my first December out there, we were waiting for our doughnuts and coffee. Allie and I and two or three of the others decided to get into the spirit of the season by singing Christmas carols. We drew our coats closer around our shivering bodies and started to sing. To put it more accurately, we tried to sing; but much to our surprise, not to say our consternation, no one could remember so much

114

as one verse of those beloved old songs. Most of us had been singing them since we were old enough to lisp the words, but that night we could not remember them. Not even Silent Night, and everyone knew Silent Night. Kindergartners make paper chains for their classroom Christmas tree and sing Silent Night as they work. We could not remember it.

We also struck out on Little Town of Bethlehem, Oh Come All Ye Faithful, and We Three Kings. Our minds remained stubbornly blank, and no one else in the yard was able to help us. We quavered along for a while, but finally gave up "Project Sing-Along" as a lost cause. I think we felt better for the trying, though, and for a few minutes at least, we forgot the cold, the dark, and the loneliness. By then it was time for donuts and coffee, after which we would wheel our carts to our various campsites. We could nestle down snugly for the night in our sleeping bags and blankets. While visions of sugarplums danced through our heads? Not this bunch; we couldn't even remember Silent Night.

For two Christmases, one group (I think it was the Adventists) brought a Christmas tree to the yard. After decorating it, they distributed gifts and serenaded us with Christmas carols, which they did not forget. Until the day after Christmas, the little tree, with its silvery tinsel dancing and shimmering in the yard lights and the breeze, reminded us that we had not been forgotten.

CHAPTER 12
TEDDY BEAR

In November of 1989, the temperature in Las Vegas dipped to near freezing. St. Vincent's was preparing to start its winter shelter program. That year, however, management had decided not to include women in the program. The Salvation Army had a seven-night stay with a six months wait until the next visit policy, which wasn't of much help to us.

The Las Vegas Rescue Mission also had a seven-night policy for women, with a 30-day waiting period. The men got even less. Their beds were assigned on a first-time, first-served basis. The repeaters got whatever beds were left if any, and the men's beds were not assigned to them until after the one-hour chapel service. One of the unforgivable sins at the Rescue Mission was falling asleep in the chapel, no matter how long one had been deprived of sleep. To break this rule was to not get a bed if one was a man, or to lose one's bed if one was a woman. It was not easy to sit comfortably for an hour without dozing off, especially when one had no rest for three days, but that was the requirement.

Anyway, that winter we women were wondering what we would do. Finally, just in time to ward off an epidemic of nervous breakdowns among us, we were told that St. Luke's Episcopal Church on Eastern Avenue, about two miles from St. Vincent's Plaza, had agreed to serve as a shelter for women and children until sometime in March. It was under the sponsorship of the Jubilee Ministry. If I remember correctly, Jubilee Ministry was an

117

activity of the Episcopal Church. On a cold, wintry night, we were driven in a St. Vincent's van to the charming little white church for our first night at St. Luke's.

Due to the suddenness of the cold spell, we had arrived at St. Luke's several nights before we had been expected, but the staff rose to the occasion and somehow managed to come up with enough hot soup and coffee for all of us. Our quarters were in the basement, where there were two restrooms and a small but well-equipped kitchen. There were also tables and chairs.

Unfortunately, we eventually pushed out the Alcoholics Anonymous group, who had been holding their meetings at St. Luke's before our intrusion. They weren't too happy about this turn of events, and I could not blame them. The church basement was a perfect meeting place. I didn't know where the AA people went from St. Luke's.

After soup and coffee, the tables and chairs were folded and put away. We were given blankets and plastic mats to make into pallets on the floor. That was to be our routine for the rest of the time we were at St. Luke's.

Jubilee Ministry ran the shelter for the first four months of its existence, with St. Vincent's providing the van and the drivers for our transportation. Some of the drivers were not very enchanted with the job of driving around a bunch of chattering women, and they were really grouchy. Others seemed to enjoy the job, and they were more congenial. One of the latter became so interested in a conversation that some women were having that much to his embarrassment, he ran a red light and found himself stuck in the middle of a wide intersection. Fortunately, traffic was light at that moment and he was able to back out of his dilemma without mishap. He was a bit less congenial after that experience, but not much.

The vans and drivers were also used to carry the

men on St. Vincent's work program to and from their jobs. This double duty meant that we sometimes had to wait until as late as seven o'clock before we could go to the shelter and eat dinner. After a long day on the street, we were already tired and hungry, and those long waits were as boring as they were wearying. Once in a while, some of the ladies managed to liven things up a bit.

One evening, one of the women was talking about the small town where she had grown up. She said that her family's burial plot was located in that town, and when she died, that was where she was going to be buried.

"I'm not going to be buried," said one of the other women. "I'm going to be cremated and have my ashes scattered. I don't want the kids to start crying when they come to the house and see the Pepsi bottle sitting on the shelf. "There's Mom, in the Pepsi bottle."

Until then, I had not thought of a Pepsi bottle as suitable material for a burial urn, but this young woman had obviously given the matter considerable thought. If the Pepsi Company ever decided to start manufacturing burial urns, I think I'd buy some stock in the company. This could have been a profitable new field for expansion. It certainly had some intriguing, creative possibilities.

Eventually, St. Luke's acquired a van, and those women on staff who had driver's licenses served as chauffeurs. It did little to improve the timing of our transportation, as those drivers were not always readily available. Indeed, there were a few times when Mrs. Christine Cole, one of the pastors at St. Luke's, provided the service for us. The women drivers were not subjected to nearly as much teasing as the men had received. As far as I knew, none of them received many proposition's either; especially not Pastor Christine.

Miss K. had an upsetting experience when we were

there. While she was outside the shelter smoking a cigarette, somebody stole Teddy Bear. Although Miss K. did
not suffer under the delusion that Teddy Bear was anything but the cute, little stuffed toy that she was to her
mistress. Teddy Bear was still the friend and companion
who would never let her down. Miss K. replied when she
was criticized for talking to a stuffed bear, "Other people
have dogs and cats to talk to; why shouldn't I have Teddy
Bear?"

Why not, indeed? Miss K. also mentioned the matter of pet rocks. Why was it any less logical to have a toy
bear for a pet than it was to have a rock for a pet? Not
even the Flintstones had a pet rock; they had a pet dino-
saur. Anyway, when Miss K. came back into the basement
and saw that her pet was gone from her basket, she started
to unravel. Although I slept next to Miss K. and Teddy
Bear, my eyes were closed and I had not seen the thief.

It was early in the evening, and most of the women
were still up and about (I went to bed unusually early). I
could not imagine how anyone could possibly have taken
the bear without somebody seeing her, but someone had
done just that. Only the week before, Miss K. had had
another unpleasant experience similar to this incident.
That time, too, she was outside the basement door smoking. Somebody got into her bedroll and stole ten dollars,
some food stamps, some toilet articles, and a charming
picture of Teddy Bear. It had been taken by a professional
photographer who visited the yard one day. As were
so many others, the photographer was intrigued by the
expression of interested alertness on the little bear's face.
He had captured it perfectly on film.

Teddy Bear had many friends, and the thought of
losing her was more than Miss K. could handle. For an
hour or more, there was a frantic search of the shelter and

the grounds surrounding the church. The street on which the property was situated was also searched, but to no avail. No trace of Teddy Bear was found, and Miss K. was becoming more upset by the minute.

Finally, after she insisted that all the people and their belongings be checked, Miss F. decided to look one more time in the restrooms, even though they had been checked a couple of times already. This time, though, her hunch paid off. Teddy Bear was in one of the wastebaskets. She was soaked. It looked as though she had been dumped in one of the toilets, but Miss K. was too happy at having her little friend back to complain very much. She just gave Teddy Bear a bath and put her to bed. Although Teddy Bear did not say so, I imagined she was happy that her ordeal was finally over and she was back with her mama. Miss F., too, was happy that she had been able to help Miss K. and Teddy Bear. It was a joyous time for all.

Well, not quite all. Another guest of the shelter, who had not been feeling well that day, became quite ill that evening. In the midst of all the excitement over the bearnapping, the paramedics were called for her.

I don't know how the bearnapper managed to get rid of the evidence without anyone seeing her. But I guess it was the same way she managed to get away with Teddy Bear in the first place. Miss K.'s insistence that everyone be searched had the desired result, all right. It got Teddy Bear back.

A day or so later, one of the staff members told Miss K. who the thief was. I don't know how they found out who she was, but if they were right. The woman had a history of mental illness. She could be very obnoxious. That was one of the problems with some mentally-ill people. One knew they were sick, but they could be so hateful that it was difficult to feel sympathy for them.

121

I also did not know how the workers in the shelters manage to cope with all their problems. One night, a woman who had not been a problem in the shelter leaped suddenly from her pallet and attacked the woman sleeping next to her. This hapless lady had done nothing to provoke the attack. I don't think she was even snoring. After losing several chunks of hair, she developed a condition for which she later had to go to the hospital for treatment. The shelter monitor on duty that night was finally able to get to the telephone and call for help.

Miss S.'s explanation for her attack on the monitor was that Mary had "interfered in my fight." I did not hear if Miss S. had an explanation for her unexpected aggression against her sleeping neighbor. Mary was not the first staff member at St. Luke's to be attacked by one of the guests. Yvonne, however, was bigger and stronger than Mary, and she was able to defend herself without injuring the aggressor. Miss S. was a large, husky young woman, and little Mary did not have a chance against her.

Between the women who were on booze or drugs, the mentally ill, and the just plain ornery, the staff members of the shelters should have gotten combat pay, but I don't think they did.

Besides the physical abuse to which they were subjected, they were also accused of all kinds of misconduct. Some of the women at St. Luke's had claimed they were kicked and kicked and kicked to wake them up in the morning. Once in a while we had a grouchy worker, but I doubted very much if they repeatedly kicked anyone. I could imagine that a worker, desperate after several futile attempts to awaken someone, might nudge a pallet or a sleeper's foot with her toe, but not kicking.

Nudging a pallet with one's foot is the safest way to wake up the average street person. It's safer than bending over and touching them with one's hand. People, who slept outdoors without protection, became very sensitive to being touched unexpectedly when asleep, and they were likely to react violently. Some of the ladies carried knives, large screwdrivers, or anything that could be used as a weapon.

I found out how sensitive and how fast they could react when I had to go to the bathroom one night. The shelter was very crowded that evening, and the mats were only a few inches apart. On my way to the bathroom, I threaded my way through the recumbent figures without incident. Before I came out of the restroom, however, one of the women stretched her legs across the narrow aisle. When I tried to step over them, I inadvertently touched one of the legs gently, but that was enough.

With something approaching the speed of light, the agile young woman flipped over onto her back and kicked me with both feet. Fortunately, she did not connect with enough force to topple me onto any of the other sleepers, and I made it back to my bed without killing or being killed.

One of the staff members at St. Luke's charitably said that the women who claimed they were kicked and kicked were hallucinating. She could be right. Some of these women had had really terrible experiences such as robberies, rapes, beatings, or abuse of one kind or another. I suppose these memories did haunt the women, especially when they were half asleep.

CHAPTER 13
A WAVE OF INTENSE LOVE

Like the story of the loaves of bread and fish in the Christian Bible, the staff at St. Luke's sometimes performed veritable miracles in keeping us fed. The people who promised to furnish our dinners were usually very faithful in keeping their promises. Occasionally, they could not make it and did not always let the staff know of this change of plans. On those occasions the staff, after waiting as long as they could for the promised meal, would pitch in and somehow manage to come up with enough food for sixty to one hundred or more women and children. I don't know how they did it. Maybe they were magicians, but we never went to bed hungry while we were at St. Luke's.

The Episcopalian ladies who initially furnished our dinners were great cooks. We had some fabulous casserole dishes among other delicacies such as soups, salads, vegetables (they even made green beans taste good to me—no easy task), meats, and desserts. It must have taken a lot of time, work, and a considerable amount of money to furnish that much food day after day. One evening I complimented one group of ladies on the meal they served and remarked on how much work it must have been.

"We don't mind," said one of the women. Then, indicating the other women in the kitchen with a wave of her hand, she added, "We're all related, and we enjoy the chance to get together."

Eventually, the Showboat Hotel and Casino and the Golden Nugget Hotel and Casino furnished our dinners several nights a week. Those meals, too, were always delicious and ample.

I had a memorable if not mysterious experience one evening while waiting for the van to take us to St. Luke's. I was half listening as some of the other women chatted among themselves or conversed with the security guards on duty. Suddenly and quite unexpectedly, a wave of intense love for everyone in the room flooded my being. It is difficult to describe, but it seemed to be a sort of protective love. I wanted to know that all those people were all right; that they would be provided for, taken care of.

Not only did I not normally love all those people, I did not know all of them. Some of those whom I did know, I did not particularly care for, and they felt the same way about me. But at that moment, I loved them all intensely and unconditionally.

"This must be the way God loves," I thought. "Maybe it is God's love, which for some reason beyond my understanding was expressing itself through me."

The sensation lasted for only a moment or so, but it left an indelible, if not always consciously remembered impression in my psyche. I wondered if this world would be changed to any appreciable degree if every human could have this experience at least once in his or her lifetime.

In March of 1990, Jubilee's contract for running the St. Luke's shelter ran out, and we resigned ourselves to once again sleeping outdoors. However, Christine and Roy Cole, the pastors of St. Luke's, were determined that would not happen. They worked very hard drumming up support for the shelter. I lost most of my notes I made at that time, and I did not remember what arrangements were made for keeping the shelter program going. But if I recall correctly, there was a cooperative effort by a number of groups. Some of the local television stations and both of the local newspapers gave a great deal of publicity to the project. There was a lot of support from the community.

I think that the City of Las Vegas also helped out, as did St. Vincent's, among others. Las Vegans did not want women and children living on the street if they could help it. All those efforts kept the shelter open until December 21, 1990, when the officials at St. Luke's decided they wanted their church back—while there was any remnant of a church left to take back.

As usual, some people would take care of the property, but others did not. I felt sorry for the building, which had once been so neat and pretty, and for those who had worked hard over a period of many years to keep it that way. There was always the same problem with trying to help the homeless. St. Luke's was no exception.

It had been a year of hard work, prayers, and a lot of scrounging on the part of the Coles and others. In the summer of 1990, Mr. and Mrs. Cole returned to their home in Texas, but they had done their work well. The year had been particularly eventful for Mrs. Cole. She had first been ordained as a deacon in the Episcopal Church in a solemn and impressive ceremony, which we had been invited to attend. After a six-month waiting period, Chris was then ordained as a priest. I imagine that ceremony was even more impressive than had been the first one. But due to a misunderstanding of the rules by one of the attendants, I did not get to attend the second ceremony.

One man, who had read or heard about the shelter, volunteered to do the maintenance work for us. An engineer who worked on the volcano at the Mirage Resort, he was willing to give up some of his free time to help. There was always plenty of work to do. Despite ongoing pleas to keep the outside door closed to protect the cooling system, most of the women refused to cooperate, and the coolers broke down repeatedly. Each time this happened, the basement became suffocatingly hot, but those women never learned. I spent so much time jumping up and down to shut the door that I felt like a yo-yo. Still I could not keep up with the almost constant stream of traffic going out and coming in the door.

The restroom plumbing was frequently clogged, and the washbowls were torn from the walls. I doubted the AA group ever treated the church that roughly, and I imagine the officials at St. Luke's wished that they had the AA people back. I didn't blame them. Before he gave up on us and quit St. Luke's in disgust, the maintenance man told us some interesting things about the volcano.

He said, for instance, that they did not dare operate the little erupter when the wind was blowing at twelve miles an hour or more because they could not, as he put it, "control the flame patterns." They had a few scorched palm trees to illustrate what he meant about not controlling the flame pattern. If you come to Las Vegas in hopes of seeing the volcano in action but are disappointed, do check the wind velocity that day before you get mad at the Mirage.

One night our dinner was served by a group of Cub Scouts. They were little fellows who could barely reach up into the soup pot. Their arms got so tired that from time to time they had to be pulled off for a few minutes. One of the youngsters had even made the tossed salad, which they served. They were darling boys.

Another night three charming little girls entertained us. When they finished singing, the little ladies pitched in. They helped put away the tables and chairs and laid the mats on the floor. We've heard so much about how terrible the youth of today are, but these two stories serve to illustrate the fact that generalizations can be tricky, and also unfair. This one was certainly unfair to the young people themselves, and to those who were nurturing and teaching them.

Some people were convinced that the American educational system had gone completely down the drain. In some spots, perhaps, but not quite completely. I didn't think these pessimists had ever watched the teen tournament on NBC television's Jeopardy program. These young people were sharp, poised, and polite. Somebody must have been doing something right. Whatever it was, it was being done by teachers who were not being paid two or three million dollars a semester for their work. Teaching has to be one of the toughest, most nerve-wracking and important jobs in the world, but our teachers have to fight bitterly for every dollar they get.

Despite what sports fans might think, and I speak as one of them, we could survive without sports. We could not survive as a civilized, progressive and great nation without a good educational system and good teachers. So much for our sense of values.

One year, the Penny Press puzzle magazines published two puzzles that had been submitted by two sixth graders, a boy and a girl. The youngsters attended a school in Washington State; I did not remember the name of the city. There was a project in their school to see if the students could get something into print: a poem, a story, a cartoon, anything. Although the class, which the boy and girl attended, was not included in that project, their teacher thought his students might enjoy a similar activity. The children were interested, and the boy and girl chose word games as the subject of their entries.

They submitted their puzzles to Penny Press

together with their story, and as said, the publisher of the magazine accepted the puzzles. The publisher also paid the young constructors at the magazines regular contributor's rate. Not yet in junior high school, these youngsters were already professionals. That does sound pretty ignorant, doesn't it?

A few years ago, a young United States spelling champion appeared on the Tonight Show. He and Johnny Carson engaged in a spelling bee of their own. That young man could spell words that I had never heard of, and I don't think that Mr. Carson had ever heard of them, either. There are so many new words being spawned every year by modern technology, only a computer could keep track of them all. And we did it with only twenty-six alphabetical characters.

It seems to me that today's school children have a great deal more to learn than we did when I went to school. I don't know how they do it all. One of my neighbors said he recently met a young American high school graduate who thought Oregon was a foreign country. I guess that shows some students don't learn it all, or even very much of it.

In spite of the optimistic statements and examples of scholastic achievement in the forgoing paragraphs, it did sound as though certain areas of our educational system could use an overhauling. This could well include some basic geography. Unless he moved to Oregon, somewhere in this country, there is a young man who will be very embarrassed if he tries to get traveling papers to go to that "foreign" country. Let us hope he was the only one. After all, he could have been absent the day the rest of his class learned about the beautiful state of Oregon.

The youth's reaction to my neighbor's explanation that Oregon was one of the fifty United States was,

"You're kidding?" My reaction to my neighbor's story was also, "You're kidding!" But he wasn't.

After several months of illness, Sarge passed away on April 14, 1990—Good Friday. As was frequently the case, when someone close to me dies, my feelings are mixed. On the one hand, Sarge, although I said that he had been ill for only a few months, had been sick for much longer than that according to Ernest. For the prior few months, however, it had been more and more obvious that something was seriously wrong with Sarge. Ernest said that our friend had been in a great deal of pain, although Sarge did not mention that fact to me. Toward the last, he became too ill to even play his beloved pinochle and was in and out of the hospital every few days. I would not want him to linger on in that misery if he could not get well.

On the other hand, we had been neighbors under the arcade roof for over a year, and Sarge was like a brother to me. He was continually doing something for me. It was Sarge who found me a shopping cart for which the cart collectors were not interested. (Cart collectors are people who round up lost, strayed, or stolen shopping carts and for a fee, return them to their owner stores. It was a lucrative business.) Sarge also managed to wheedle a chair out of someone at St. Vincent's that he gave to me. It was also Sarge who found and brought to me the large piece of plastic to protect my possessions and me from the rain, which still got to us even in the shelter of the arcade.

Occasionally, I was able to repay Sarge for some of his kindness by doing a sewing job for him. I missed him very much. It did not seem right that someone else now occupied the spot that Sarge once defended so assiduously. Hughie had known Sarge for many years, and I know that seeing his friend go so rapidly downhill nearly broke Hughie's heart. How I regret those times when I was cross with Sarge for swishing dirt on my breakfast and me.

On the mornings when the cleanup crew had not cleaned his "house" to suit him, Sarge took an old shirt or sweater and swished his floor clean over and over. Unfortunately for me, I was usually having my daily bowl of cereal at that time, and my finicky friend swished his dirt right onto my cereal and me. When I protested, he told me brusquely to move. By that time, I had usually already moved once and did not have many more places to move to. Sarge was a vigorous swisher, and we were in a crowded area. My options were limited.

However, my vocabulary was not limited. In retaliation for his actions, I gave him my unsolicited and uncensored opinions of him and his behavior. As I recall, "selfish, crude, inconsiderate," and "jerk" were a few of them. I did not have the faintest idea at that time that Sarge would be leaving us so soon. Forgive me, Sarge, I didn't mean it! We should live each day as though family and friends would be gone tomorrow. Sometimes, they are.

Pain can make us grouchy. That surly treatment, so unlike Sarge's normal attitude toward me, might have been the result of pain he was in. Before he got so sick, Sarge did not spend all his time curmudgeoning. He had his little jokes. For instance, when one of the men (there weren't many women in that area) had done something he felt was especially meritorious, Sarge would nudge me in the ribs with his elbow and whisper with a wink, "That was white of him." Sarge's complexion was quite dark—really almost black—and that remark never failed to break me up.

On May 3rd, a memorial service for the homeless people who died the preceding year was held at St. James

Church on Las Vegas's west side. St. James was an attractive, well-kept neighborhood church. The congregation was very active in helping the homeless people of this area. Brother Harry, a Franciscan Monk who also worked closely with homeless people, conducted the service. He did it with beauty, dignity, and feeling. Brother Harry was such a nice man. Seeing Sarge's name at the head of the list of the departed, which was printed in the program we were given, undid me. But I was not the only one who wept, albeit silently, through most of the service. The people being remembered were friends and associates.

Some, like Sarge, had died of natural causes, but several had been murdered. One of the latter was a quiet young man who was brutally stabbed and bludgeoned to death in the very camp Risa and I had been sleeping in before St. Luke's opened. We got out of that camp just in time.

One man was remembering three members of his family who had passed away back East that year. Mr. B. felt so badly at not being able to attend their funerals that he asked for them to be included in this service. They were. Despite its poignant reminder of Sarge's passing, there was a certain comfort in being able to attend the memorial service that included him. None of us had known where he had been taken the last time the paramedics came to the yard for him.

That time he had not wanted to leave his camp, but he was very weak and sick—too sick even to get to a restroom, someone said. We could not take proper care of him out there, although some of the men had been trying to do just that. We learned that Sarge had gone to a rest home, only because someone from the home called St. Vincent's to notify them he had passed away.

Sarge had passed from our lives without our having

had a chance to say goodbye to him. In a way, the memorial service had given me a chance to do that. Hughie did not attend the service—I guess he felt that he could not bear it—but he had been a faithful visitor during Sarge's several stays in a hospital. That was more than I had done. Hughie had nothing to atone for.

CHAPTER 14
FAMOUS FOR BEING POOR

Once again, and without realizing it at the time, we women got out of the way of danger—even if it was only the danger of being scared to death. One morning, when we got back to the yard from St. Luke's, the man told us that the night before, the police chased someone through the camp we had been sleeping in. This time the cops had dogs with them, and they were firing their guns into the air.

Apparently, no one was either shot by the officers or bitten by the dogs, but the homeless were not always so fortunate. That latest incident did not sound to me as much like a chase as it did simple harassment; like trying to scare some people out of town. It worked for Hughie. I heard him say that he was going to another state to snatch a dull moment. They don't have to work that hard to get rid of me. I'd been trying to get out of this situation for some time; I just hadn't made it yet.

For years, I maintained an informal and totally futile war with the television industry, despite my impassioned defense of the medium in my "debates" with Sarge and Emory. Not that I had anything against television per se; I thought it was a fantastic development in human history. It was just that in my present circumstances, I did not need all that exposure. I blamed an interview, taped and broadcast by one of the local stations, for the beating of my friend, John.

The interview was conducted by a police officer, but recorded by the television crew also in the field that night. It attracted some unwelcome attention in the neighborhood, which resulted in John's beating a night or two later. Certain elements in the area resented something that was said in the interview, and they rushed our camp in reprisal. The broadcast must also have called attention to the condition of the field, which was not a pretty sight. A few nights after the airing of the interview, the police met us when we started to push our carts across Main Street to the field. The officers informed us that we were no longer allowed to sleep in that location.

We heard later that the company, which managed the property for the absentee owners, said that they would not mind if we slept there, but it was too costly to keep the campsite cleaned up. I don't remember where we went that time. We did not necessarily live in a vacuum, simply because we did not have a conventional home, either. We transacted business in town, shopped at neighborhood stores, patronized banks and libraries, and spent money in the casinos. Even when they were doing nothing wrong, however, people who were known to be homeless are run out of the casinos and viewed with suspicion in other places. It could be very embarrassing.

Metro also kept a watchful eye on us. We would just as soon they did not recognize us as homeless persons when they saw us. So many times, just before something was done to us, it seemed as though a crew from one of the local television stations had been seen in our vicinity not long before. As a result of this, we had begun to think of television as the enemy, on par with Metro. This opinion began to change for me, however, after we women started going to St. Luke's.

It was during that period that Nita, the woman who had been interviewed in the field, chanced to meet the reporter who was part of the television crew that night.

The reporter recognized Nita and told her that she felt so sorry for the women in the field. I guess television was not necessarily the enemy after all—not intentionally, anyway.

Despite its sometimes-negative impact on the homeless, the extensive coverage did have its positive aspects. The publicizing of the hardships endured by those without homes resulted in a great deal of community support for the soup kitchens and homeless shelters. People did remember what they saw and heard on television. Some of my experiences testified to that fact.

One charming lady, who sometimes volunteered to work at St. Vincent's as a server on the lunch line, had two standard greetings for me when I approached her station. One of them was, "I saw you on television." The other one was, "I haven't seen you on television."

The second comment was made in almost an accusatory tone, as though I had somehow let her down when I did not show up on her television screen regularly. She was so cute and friendly, not at all snooty or superior, that I had to laugh. After all, a fan was a fan and should be appreciated.

One evening, as we were waiting to get into St. Vincent's annex shelter, I told the woman in line behind me about my friend on the serving line. She laughed and said, "You're becoming famous for being homeless." A dubious distinction, but I guess she was right.

Quite a number of years ago, the Triple A Hotel was closing. A local television station must have thought it was a newsworthy event because a cameraman and a reporter visited the dormitory where I was packing my belongings. They asked if they could record the packing process. Without thinking of the possible consequences, I answered, "Sure, go ahead."

The next day I was playing Keno in a downtown casino when the Keno writer asked me, "Didn't I see you on television last night?" Embarrassed I answered, "Oh, I suppose so." I needn't have felt embarrassed that time, though. Without having asked me any questions about my intentions, the reporter had assumed that I had a place to go, and had so stated on the broadcast. I did not consider it necessary to tell the friendly Keno writer that the place I went to was the Greyhound bus station, where I stashed my bags in a locker. I think I got a live-in job after that.

Some of my friends, too, remarked about seeing me in "living color," referring to a particularly colorful blouse I was wearing at the time of the move. I think what finally turned my attitude toward television around was an interview I did with Mike Raddig for Channel 5. At the request of a woman who worked at both St. Luke's and Friendship Corner, I wrote an article for the *HAPpenings* paper.

Utterly by coincidence—I did not even think of the tie with Friendship Corner—I chose friendships on the street as the theme for my article. Mike, who at that time was both the director of Friendship Corner and the editor of *HAPpenings*, liked the article. After printing it in his paper, he asked me if I would mind if he took it to Mr. Mike O'Callahan of the Las Vegas Sun newspaper. Mike Raddig and I had a sort of gentlemen's agreement about the friendship article. He agreed that I could use it in my book if I wanted to, and I agreed that he could take it to Mr. O'Callahan if that was what he wanted to do. That was what he did, and Mr. O'Callahan printed it in the Sun's "Where I Stand" column. The interview at Channel 5 followed. It was Mike Raddig's hope that the broadcast would somehow help the homeless cause. That's why I agreed to do it, although I had my usual misgivings about the publicity.

I don't know whether we helped our cause or not, but the interview did not bring hordes of producers rushing to the yard with lucrative contracts for me to sign. The program might not have impressed the television producers, and I didn't really think it would—especially not at 5:30 in the morning. But I did get proof that some people had watched the broadcast.

The lovely young lady at Channel 5 who conducted the interview made me feel right at home. I was not at all nervous. I guess it showed. The interview was taped around noon for airing early the next morning. When we women got home from St. Luke's the morning of the broadcast, I was greeted by a woman who must have been visiting the yard from someplace else, as there was no way she could have seen the program otherwise. Anyway, she told me she had seen the broadcast; just that, and nothing more. How had I done? Had people thought I was fairly interesting? Or had they turned off their sets until I was off the air, as I do when someone bores me? Clearly I was not going to get the answer to my questions from that viewer. I did not want to sound as though I was fishing for compliments, so I did not press her for an opinion.

I learned little more from a male acquaintance whom I met as I proceeded farther into the yard. He too was visiting the yard that day. I knew that he no longer lived there, and he also had seen the broadcast. Since I knew Martin fairly well, I could not resist the temptation to ask him how I had done.

"All right," was his laconic reply. Damning with faint praise? At least he hadn't turned his television set off on me; that was encouraging. Indeed, things did pick up somewhat after that. Another visitor to the yard later in the morning was positively enthusiastic about both my appearance and my performance.

So, too, was a charming lady, obviously also of good taste (although a stranger to me). She stopped at my table in a neighborhood fast-food restaurant a day or so later. I thought it was so gracious of her to take the time to stop and compliment a total stranger on something she had done. I was really very moved.

Then Erynne, who was the manager of the Shade Tree shelter for women, told me that I came across on television as being "warm and sincere." I decided that I was going to put the rave reviews in my memory book. What do the others know? Their remarks also proved that people remember what they see and hear on television, even if they see and hear it at 5:30 in the morning.

Anyway, as a result of all this electronic activity, I decided to drop my feud with the television industry. I was acting on the philosophy that if you can't lick 'em, you might as well join 'em. No one in the industry had noticed the feud, anyway, so at best it was just an exercise in futility; and heaven knows I didn't need any more of that.

Miss F. had to be one of the country's outstanding telephone salespersons, even if she didn't think so. Ever so often, when she needed to earn some money (her health does not permit her to work full-time), Miss F. took a job for a few days or a few weeks in telemarketing. One year she was selling subscriptions to a local newspaper with some surprising results.

When making calls from her list of prospects, she noticed that one of the names looked familiar. She gave the matter no thought, however, until she got well into her sales pitch. Then she realized, to her embarrassment, that the man she was talking to was the circulation manager for the very newspaper she was trying to sell him. She immediately tried to terminate the call. Not only would the man not hear of it, he insisted that the flustered Miss F. put him down for a subscription to the paper. "But, Mr. Manager," Miss F. persisted, "while I do not advocate stealing, I'm sure the publisher would not mind if you picked up a paper on the way home from work."

Mr. Manager was a good sport, however, and refused to cancel his order. Maybe the publisher did mind if his employees picked up a paper on the way home from work. Miss F. never found out. She got quite a different reaction when she called another prospect, although the end result was the same. When she told that man the purpose of her call, he hit the ceiling.

"I hate that paper," he fumed. "I can't stand the publisher. Every time I pick up the paper, his family's pictures are plastered all over it. I can't stand that paper."

After such a tirade as that, I would have hung up the phone and not had the nerve to make another call for a week, if ever. But Miss F. was undaunted. "Look at it this way, Mr. Prospect," she said soothingly. "You get up in the morning, shower and shave, and as you're eating breakfast, you read the paper. You get all your ill nature out of your system. By the time you get to the office, you are all smiles, and your co-workers think you are the nicest guy in the place."

By this time the prospect was laughing. He was so amused by this novel presentation that he, too, bought a subscription to the paper, even though he still did not like the publisher. Heaven help the Eskimos if Miss F. ever decided to sell refrigerators.

On November 30, 1990, as we were eating our dinner, the blow we had for so long been dreading, finally came. We were told that this would be our last night at St. Luke's. The church officials wanted their church back, probably while there was still some shred of a church left to take back. For the more nervous among us, of whom I was always one, it was panic time again. Where would we go from here? I would not have minded sleeping in St. Vincent's yard, but for security reasons, women were not allowed in the yard at night. St. Vincent's remained adamant in their refusal to shelter women inside that year.

After being kept in suspense for what seemed like an eternity, we were finally told that the Salvation Army had agreed to take us in until the new twenty-four-hour shelter for women and children, The Shade Tree, was ready for occupancy. They expected to accomplish this within a few weeks.

A building adjacent to St. Vincent's Plaza had been acquired by St. Vincent's and was being converted to the shelter. St. Vincent's, however, would not be running the shelter. That job would be done by Jubilee Ministry, the same Jubilee Ministry that had managed the St. Luke's shelter. Our first night at the Salvation Army was on December 1st. Their women's shelter could not accommodate such a large influx of women and children, and the overflow were given mats and blankets and bedded down in the dining room. We felt right at home there.

We had been moved from hither to yon and back again so many times that I felt like a pawn on a chessboard. I had lost track of the sequence of some of our earlier moves when I was not taking notes on our peregrinations. We were, however, still sleeping inside, and we got our breakfast before starting out in the morning. So once again, we were being taken care of.

This happy state of affairs was not destined to last forever, though. After putting up with us for a couple of weeks or so, our unwilling hosts informed Jubilee that as of December 20th, they were ending their emergency shelter program. If Jubilee was not ready for us, we would be out in the cold; and it was cold in Las Vegas that winter. Daytime temperatures hovered around freezing. For several years, we had been experiencing the coldest winters I had ever seen in this area, and that was one of them.

Although work on the reconstruction of the building had preceded apace, The Shade Tree still did not have all its foliage in place. Jubilee was not prepared for us. Only part of the bunk beds had been assembled, the restrooms were not completed, the executive offices were not yet finished, and there was heat only in the dormitories. The large dayroom, the entry hall, the monitor's desk area, and the restroom area were cold; like wearing your coat, hat and mittens indoors cold.

However, because most of the women were not equipped for sleeping outdoors, Jubilee once again agreed to take us in, ready or not. The Shade Tree had received a great deal of publicity from the media, and the mayor of Las Vegas himself cut the ribbon at the ceremony, which kicked off the new shelter. He nearly froze, too.

Many of the good people of Las Vegas, moved by the plight of homeless women and children, braved the cold to bring Christmas gifts of food, clothing, toilet articles, toys, and other items to the shelter. So we had a pleasant Christmas, even if it was a shivery one. A shelter, which would be open twenty-four hours so women and children could stay inside during the day as well as night, had long been a dream of Jubilee's. They were at last seeing the dream come true.

A few years ago, a man wrote a letter to a local "Letters to the Editor" column. In it he said that he could face the enemy, but that seeing women and children on the street got to him. I guess a lot of people felt the way that man did. Although there was a microwave oven and a refrigerator in the dayroom, which the shelter guests were allowed to use, the Shade Tree had no kitchen. Any food that was left in the refrigerator was not always there when one went back for it; not even milk that some mother had intended for her baby.

At the time I stayed at the shelter, breakfast was the only meal served at The Shade Tree, unless some church group brought in a meal and served it. Usually, however, breakfast consisted of dry cereal, coffee, and milk, when there was milk. If there was no milk, even the children had to put black coffee on their cereal. Black coffee was not a tasty substitute for milk or cream.

CHAPTER 15
ON THE STREET OF PEEVES

I heard that Shade Tree now had one or two showers; not enough for sixty or more people, so most of the women and children still had to go to St. Vincent's at 1:30 in the afternoon to take their daily shower. A shower each day was a requirement for holding one's bed at the shelter. That was also true of the Salvation Army and the Las Vegas Rescue Mission, but they had their own showers.

At Shade Tree, however, any woman who had any kind of an appointment at 1:30 p.m.—doctor's appointment, job interview, welfare or food stamp appointment, whatever—and could not make it down the hill for her shower had a problem. She had to present an affidavit at the shelter to the effect that she attended the appointment. Not only was that embarrassing for the woman, but sometimes it was downright impossible.

People did not want to behave like a mother writing an excuse for a truant child, and some prospective employers would not hire anyone who lived at a shelter. The women were reluctant to ask a potential employer to provide a written excuse for missing a shower. I did not know what these ladies did. The shelter was supposed to be helping women to get on their economic feet; it was not supposed to be making the situation even more difficult for them. A guest of Shade Tree did, however, get to eat dinner at St. Vincent's with the people who stayed there, as well as with the guests of St. Vincent's new family shelter, The Crossroads. These meals were complete, from salad to dessert, and were always excellent.

Although it was dedicated to helping people, the course of Shade Tree was not destined to run with absolute smoothness. On the morning of January 4th, while most of the women were still in the dormitories, a car running out of control down the Main Street hill crashed through the west wall of one of the dormitories. The bunks were lined up along the north and south sides of the rooms. Miss F.'s bunk and my bunk were the first two beds next to the west wall, across the center aisle from each other.

The automobile narrowly missed Miss F., who was standing at the foot of her bed, and made a beeline for my bed. It pushed my bunk into the bunk of Miss K., who slept next to me, then shoved her bed into the bed of the woman who slept on the other side of her. That car was really traveling. Miss K. and Teddy Bear were not injured, and neither was their neighbor.

Fortunately, I had been out all night playing the slot machines and had not come home yet, so I missed all the excitement. Good for me! I didn't need to be all that excited. The slot machines could be expensive, but they weren't likely to get me killed.

As much as I deplored my gambling habit, that was the second time that being out playing the slots saved me from possible injury. The first incident occurred when I was living at the Triple A Hotel. A fire broke out in the hotel one morning at about the same time of day as the accident at Shade Tree. It was two weeks to the day and about the hour of the MGM Grand fire. Between 7:00 and 7:30 in the morning seemed to be a particularly hazardous time of day in Las Vegas.

At the time of the Triple A Hotel fire, I had also been out all night. That time I was playing penny slots at Club Bingo on Fremont Street, which was only a few blocks from the hotel. But I did not hear about the fire until several hours after it was over. Although the one-story hotel was gutted, only one man, not quite sober, got his feet burned slightly when he walked toward the fire instead of away from it. The structure was originally built to serve as an overnight shelter for train crews making the changeover in Las Vegas before proceeding on to California. It was a low, barracks-type building with windows close to the ground. The windows could be climbed out of without facing a long leap, and that was what some people did.

Margaret was working as a desk clerk at the hotel on the day shift and was just coming on duty when she noticed the fire. She rushed at once to get a fire extinguisher, but the fire moved too fast. She could not stop it. She suffered from smoke inhalation and had to go to a hospital for treatment. At the hospital she was not warned against swallowing oxygen, so she swallowed the oxygen and got the bends. She felt miserable for a few days. Now, she was understandably nervous about sleeping in shelters, especially with outside doors that could not be easily opened by pushing on a bar from inside the door. She would sleep in a field before she would stay in such a shelter.

At Shade Tree, we were originally allowed ninety days on the emergency winter shelter program (the normal staying time is thirty days). However, since funding was provided for the men's shelter at St. Vincent's through May 31st, funding was also forthcoming for the women for the same period of time. Once again we were thrown a lifeline, just in the nick of time.

Four times within a few years, I was sure I was getting off the street. On one such occasion, I planned on joining some members of my family in California, but that proved not to be feasible at the time. When Allie got her van, we made arrangements for me to share it with her for a while, something that for several years she had said she wanted to do. As I had waited in the yard on that Saturday morning, Allie had agreed to pick me up. She must have changed her mind about our deal because she never arrived. I didn't find out why, but I did not make it off the street that time, either.

My third attempt at living a civilized, indoor life involved two women whom I met at Shade Tree. At the time we became acquainted, H. and M. were negotiating for the rental of a house. They invited me to share the house with them and their two daughters. M.'s daughter was a bouncy teenager. H.'s daughter was a sweet young lady in her twenties who had been ill for many years with brain cancer. I felt so sorry for her and her mother. I thought that if we lived together, I could help with J.'s care. Our time at Shade Tree was up before H. and M. got their house.

They did not contact me at the Salvation Army, where I went next, as we had agreed they would do. I neither saw nor heard from them for a couple of years or so. In the meantime, H.'s daughter passed away. Again the two women offered to share a prospective place with me, but again they were a no show. I have not seen them or heard from them since, so perhaps they went back to Hawaii as they had said they might.

As depressing as these disappointments were at the time, I was probably better off not trying to live with someone else. I really would rather have my own place. Also, if I had left the street at any of these points, I would have had even less of a book than I have now. It would have been a little more than a brochure on the art of surviving on the street. These were the thoughts with which I comforted myself, anyway.

Eternal vigilance was the price we paid for holding on to our possessions out here. One night, after we women had gone to the shelter for the night, a man appropriated my chair. The next morning, Archie and Sarge saw him bringing the chair through the gate on his shopping cart. "Mary!" Archie exclaimed. "Isn't that your chair with the crack in it?"

I could not see well enough to see the crack and positively identify the chair as mine. When I confronted the thief, he insisted that he had had the chair for a couple of months (he was a liar as well as a thief). I could not do much more than go back to my friends and tell them what had happened. At least that was all I thought I could do, but not Sarge. Without saying a word to me, he marched over to the offender, and in a few moments, he came back with the chair.

He did not say what kind of an argument he used to accomplish the feat, but I guess that defying a fragile, little old lady and defying a tough, combat-trained sergeant were two entirely different matters. I didn't know whether that man had ever been in the armed services or not. He looked like a wimp, and he was obviously no match for Sarge, although he was younger.

Sarge's performance must have been quite impressive, because not only did the man give up the chair, but also later in the day, he came to our camp and apologized to Sarge. He did not apologize to me or even look at me. But I was too happy having my chair back to give more than a passing thought to this oversight.

Another time, long after Sarge had passed away, the rest of my support group had largely scattered. I came down from the showers one afternoon to find a man, also a stranger to me, sitting in my chair. Quietly and politely, I asked him if I could have my chair. "Oh, is this your chair?" he asked.

Still with determined politeness, although I could feel the adrenalin beginning to flow, I assured him that the chair had been mine for some time. The man continued to look me in the eyes as he said with deliberate insolence, "I don't think so."

It was instant fury; the adrenalin overflowed. Forgetting that I was only a fragile, little old lady, determined not to use strong language, I hit the arcade roof. "You get out of my chair, now!" I bellowed, "or I'll have half the yard on you." I had never been angrier in my life. The nerve of the man!

Not about to admit that I had intimidated him, the intruder continued to sit in the chair for a moment. I wondered if I would have to try to make good on my threat or if I should just hit him over the head with my umbrella. Eventually, the man must have decided that half the yard presented higher odds than one old lady, and with all the speed of an arthritic snail, he arose from the chair and strolled away. Even his stroll was insolent and defiant, but at least I had my chair.

Not wanting to show my immense relief at this peaceful outcome to our little altercation, I contented myself with glaring at the man's unrepentant back. I returned the chair to its accustomed place and sat down. Thanks for the lesson, Sarge. You would have been proud of me.

If I seemed to have overreacted to the incidents of the chair, it was only because a chair was important to me. Some of the yard residents would sit or lay on their pallets during the day, but arthritic knees and hips made sitting flat a very uncomfortable position for me. I needed to sit up higher. Chairs were not that easy to come by, either, and I was not very good at scrounging.

For lunch one day, instead of soup we had spaghetti.

As usual, I had to wash my face after eating the pasta. The spaghetti was good enough, but wouldn't it taste just as good if the noodles were two inches long instead of being twelve inches long, or whatever they were?

Another of my pet peeves was "crunchy." "Crunchy" gives me both a headache and a sore mouth. Even the once melt-in-your-mouth graham crackers have joined the crunchy craze. When these crackers were dunked, they disintegrated and could not be picked up even with a spoon.

While I am on the subject of peeves, why must everything be perfumed? I used detergent in my kitchen as well as in the bathroom and the laundry, and I didn't want my food to taste and smell like perfume. I didn't need perfumed toilet tissue to make me happy, either. Maybe I would go into politics and run for president on a platform of shorter spaghetti, naturally soggy crackers, and things that just smelled clean. If this sounded like Mr. Andy Rooney, and it does, I could do worse.

Hughie was given a book of riddles, puns and stories. That particular morning, one of the other men read it to us. It has been said that a pun was the lowest form of wit, but I do not agree with that statement. To me, a good pun is a thing of beauty and a laugh forever. Dennis G. did not seem to agree with me on this.

Inspired by Hughie's book, I was doing a little punning of my own when Dennis grumped, "Don't you have someplace to go, preferably to another planet?" I had no such plans at the moment, but Dennis might just have been getting even with me for telling him he has a caustic wit. He just proved it. Of course it might just have been that Dennis really hated puns. I did not necessarily believe that accusing a person of having a caustic wit was an insult; I thought it was funny. Not everyone could manage being witty and caustic at the same time. It was an art, and Dennis was good at it. I admired him.

CHAPTER 16
MAYBE WE LAUGHED TO KEEP FROM CRYING

As much as I had hoped it would be, 1991 would not be the year to see me getting off the street. Once again we were guests of Shade Tree. This time we were there under the auspices of the St. Vincent's Winter Emergency Program. Now my hopes were pinned on 1992, and it had to be the magic year because I was running out of steam. This healthful outdoor life was aging me fast.

The senior citizens' complex that I wanted to get into had not been taking applications since last December. They were not planning on doing so until the coming August. Hopefully I could get in then. It was a nice place. I was familiar with the neighborhood, and I had friends living there.

A number of improvements had been made in the Shade Tree since I last stayed there. Coin-operated washers and dryers had been installed in the lavatory area, and they were busy day and night. Lockers, where we could keep some of our possessions, had been placed in the dormitories. They did play a little game here, which no one but its creator understood.

One day the announcement was made that after dinner, we would be given new lockers. Wondering what the new lockers would be like, we hurried from the dining room to the dormitories to clean out our old lockers, as we had been instructed to do. But where were the new lockers? All we saw were the same old ones, and that was all there were. "Getting a new locker", as it turned out, meant merely that we were to exchange lockers with some of the other women. The locks were in the doors and could not be removed. That meant that at least one other woman would know the combination of our lock—not a great idea.

We called this fact to the attention of the young lady who was in charge of Project Locker Exchange, but there was nothing she could do about the situation. It had not been her idea. It must have been the brainchild of Ms. Joyce Westcott, the director of the shelter, but Ms. Westcott was not available that evening for either question or complaint.

The best suggestion the monitor could come up with was that we find someone we could trust and exchange lockers with her. I was fortunately able to do that; rather, someone found me. I knew that others could get into our lockers because two packages of new pens had been stolen from my locker. I was lucky that only the pens had been taken, or so I told myself, but the fact that someone could get into my locker any time they wanted was upsetting. Any time a woman had used one of the lockers, she could get into it the next time she stayed at the shelter if she remembered the lock combination. The situation did not need aggravation from management to make it even worse than it already was, but we got it anyway. We never did find out why.

The roof still leaked in spots, even though it had been worked on, and some of the beds had to be moved if it rained very hard. Buckets and blankets were placed in strategic places in an effort to control any probability of flooding. This was the situation in the single women's dormitory, anyway. I did not know about the family dorm.

I didn't stay around the shelter much during the day. It was crowded and noisy, and there was no convenient place where I could write. If we went to the restroom or to St. Vincent's for lunch or showers, we had better take with us whichever belongings we were toting around that day. If we didn't, the chances were very good that they would not be there when we got back. For that reason, I tried to maintain a spot in St. Vincent's yard to stay there during the day.

We heard a generous Las Vegas woman, who was concerned about homeless people, had recently built furnished arcades along the north and the east fences and down the center of the yard. There I could sit and write. It was the next best thing to having my own place. Here, too, we watched each other's possessions. Some of us did, anyway, and our belongings were safer out there than they were at the Shade Tree. This referred to the items that we were allowed to keep in the yard. Articles kept in shopping carts in an area outside the fence were a different matter. They weren't safe at all.

My spot under the arcade was also considerably quieter than was the Shade Tree. I was also not in imminent danger of being run over by a child on a tricycle, or of being hit in the head by a basketball.

Las Vegas finally had a shelter for married couples that had children with them. The Crossroads was a project of St. Vincent's. It was located in a building on the west side of St. Vincent's Plaza, across the alley from the Shade Tree on the north. Before St. Vincent's acquired it, it was in that alley that we had one of our camps. Here, a quiet young man named Lee had been brutally slain one night, shortly after we women had started going to St. Luke's.

That was also where we were camping when our dear Thomas spent part of his nights seeing to it that we were well covered against the chill of the autumn nights. Here, too, a persistent blanket thief had finally managed to snatch a blanket to cover his "frigging arms." We were also located in that alley when a party of police officers rousted us out of bed one night.

The officers were looking for a murder suspect who had twice slipped through their fingers that week. Once they had him cornered in the yard, and that night they were in no mood for fun and games. Under the threat of shooting us if we removed our hands from the wall, they held us spread-eagle against the building, which was now the Shade Tree, while they searched us for weapons.

The suspect was not among us that night, and eventually the police left, taking with them a few men who had outstanding warrants. After they left, Thomas and some of the other men went into a huddle, during which they decided to turn the suspect in to the police. Not that night obviously, as the man was not there, but I suppose the next time he showed up in the yard. However, the fugitive was caught a few days later at another location. We heaved a collective sigh of relief.

Another episode that took place in that camp ruined forever my enjoyment of crime dramas. One night a man was kidnapped off the street near a neighborhood bar and was brought to our camp. There the luckless man was beaten and robbed. Having been asleep, I knew nothing of the kidnapping. But when I woke up to go to the bathroom, Risa, who slept next to me, hissed, "Stay down!"

I laid back down and for what seemed like a lifetime, I listened in horrified helplessness to the terrible thing that was being done to that poor man. In the darkness I could not see who his assailants were. It was probably safer that way. Take it from me; like war, real crime is nowhere nearly as entertaining as is fictionalized crime. Yes, that alley was full of memories for me, but now children from the Shade Tree and the Crossroads play there in blissful ignorance of the alley's violent and sometimes tragic past.

As careful as the management of the Crossroads was to insure the virtue of their guests, one couple fooled them. One morning, those of us who were staying at the Shade Tree were informed the dayroom would be closed to us for part of the afternoon. A wedding would take place there at that time. Actually, the room would only be partly closed to us, as we were invited to attend the ceremony if we cared to do so.

I did not attend the event, and some of us wondered who would have wanted to have a wedding at the Shade Tree. We got our answer sometime later when we learned an unmarried couple had managed to slip into the Crossroads without anyone noticing that they did not belong there. We did not hear the details, but I imagined the couple was told that they would have to get married or they would have to leave the shelter. I hope the happy couple were still happily married and in better circumstances than they must have been at the time of their wedding.

There was so much wit in this humanity that it could be one of our outstanding traits. Even those you would least expect to display an unusual amount of wit were the ones who didn't have all that much to laugh about. Maybe we laughed for one of the classic reasons given for laughing—to keep from crying.

Be that as it may, one of the women staying in the single women's dorm at this time was especially gifted in the art of standup comedy. When Judy was on a roll, she had half the dormitory in hysterics; the other half was too far away to hear. It was a very large room.

Unfortunately, there were times when the Muse of Creative Humor visited Judy after the lights were out and we were supposed to be asleep. This provoked some friction between her and me one night, when I was quite ill and was trying to get to sleep before midnight. "It isn't as though we have to get up at five o'clock," she defended herself.

I don't remember what time we did have to get up, but it was plenty early enough for me, especially that morning. Usually, I just went into hysterics along with the others. Actually, no one was supposed to come into the shelter in the middle of the night and wake up the other residents, but Judy got away with it.

One evening, I inadvertently furnished some laughter myself, although it was well before curfew. Several of the women were discussing food when the discussion got around to the parts of animals they had eaten. There was the not uncommon heart, liver, brain, even tongue. Then one woman made an announcement that I thought startled all of us. I knew it surprised me. She said that she had once eaten the penis of a cow. Before I knew what was coming, I heard myself blurt out, "That sounds like a lot of bull to me."

The laughter, which greeted that remark, did not die down completely until the lights were turned out for the night and the dormitory was supposed to be quiet. For a while, anyway, we forgot the problems that brought us to the shelter. Life in the dormitory was not all fun and games. The bunks were long enough and wide enough to be comfortable, but some of them were not very high. As a result of this, the serenity of the dorm was occasionally punctuated by a not so ladylike oath as one of the ladies bumped her head on the bunk above her. A bump on the head notwithstanding, however, inside was still better than outside. We were grateful for the shelter.

Wit was not confined to the street and the shelters. In addition to his other talents, my father was a very witty man. He said what I still think was one of the funniest lines I ever heard. We were driving into town from our home in the suburbs one day when we passed a large, buff-colored apartment building. "My!" I exclaimed, "that building certainly stands out, doesn't it?" "Probably because there isn't room enough for it inside," Dad quipped.

Dad wasn't much of a hand for cussing. In all his eighty-four years, I heard him use strong language only once. When I was about six years old, we moved to another neighborhood. The new house did not have central heating, so Dad had to set up a coal-burning stove in the combination living room/dining room/kitchen; one big room.

Dad was a master carpenter and hardly inept with his hands, but that stovepipe had a mind of its own. No sooner would Dad get it in place than it would fall down, scattering soot all over the place. About the third time this happened, even Dad's well-trained patience snapped and he erupted with a heartfelt, "D—-!"

I don't know what Mother was muttering under her breath, but probably something stronger than "d—-." Mother had had three older brothers to teach baby sister their version of the English language, while Dad had three older sisters to help bring him up in ways of gentleness. My dad's parents never cussed. "By jingoes!" was Grandfather Porter's idea of using strong language, and I don't think that any of Grandmother Porter's family cussed.

Some of the Truaxs were a little more earthy, but not Grandmother Truax. Like Grandmother Porter, Grandmother Truax was a gentlewoman, Aunt Minnie Truax, mother's older sister, did not swear, either. In fact, I think Aunt Minnie would have self-destructed before she would have said as much as "darn." To the end of her life on earth (eighty-five years), she was a devout Baptist and a spinster. She used to say that she just never met the man she wanted to marry. I think she was married to the church and its Lord.

Actually, I had two Aunt Minnie Truax's. Uncle Alf, mother's oldest brother, married a sweet and gentle lady also named Minnie. She did not cuss, either. Neither did my brother and sister. I guess mother and I were the mavericks in our family.

It was the sister Aunt Minnie who was indirectly responsible for the pen name I chose. One day, after my graduation from high school, my aunt was lamenting the fact that the Truaxs had never done very much. "Well, Aunt Minnie," I said, "if I ever get to writing, I'll write under the name 'Truax.'" I would never forget my father's love and his many sacrifices for me either, so I combined the two surnames. It took me a long time to keep that promise, but for what it's worth, Aunt Minnie, here it is.

Actually, the Truaxs were wonderful people who bore a heavy burden of sorrow and hardship with grace and humor. I don't know how they did it. Quite a number of years ago, I met a man from London. In the course of one of our conversations, I mentioned my varied ethnic background, which ranged from northern Italy through Switzerland and France, to England and Scotland.

The Englishman's reaction to this bit of personal trivia was, "Blimey! A bloomin' League o' Nytions." For six hundred years, his ancestors had been pure Cockney. It was this man who, without realizing it, taught me that the Cockney people really do talk like that; they aren't just putting it on. Up until that time, I don't think I had met a Cockney person, except in the movies, and I did not know whether the moviemakers knew what they were doing or not. I guess they did.

On Thanksgiving day of 1991, the homeless women and children of Las Vegas were again invited to the Hard Rock Café for a traditional Thanksgiving feast; and feast it was. That year the band played Christmas carols as we dined. The carols were played as proficiently as had been the rock music of the prior year. For grace, a lady vocalist sang the Ave' Maria so beautifully that I thought not even diva Marian Anderson would not have felt ashamed of the rendition.

The audience was spellbound by it. Not a whisper, not a cough disturbed the performance. I don't think we even breathed until the singer had finished, then the applause was loud and prolonged. As usual, we were treated like queens. Those lovely people made us feel as though we were doing them the favor, instead of it being the other way around. The employees of the Hard Rock Café could give lessons in gracious giving.

As we were preparing to drive out of the driveway on our way back to town, just as it had happened last year, a busload of veterans was driving in. My friend, Paddy, told me later that the veterans had been given the same red carpet treatment that had been accorded the women. He, too, mentioned the gracious service.

CHAPTER 17
THE BEAUTIFUL FLOWER OF FRIENDSHIP

This had been an eventful day, starting with the morning, when I asked Dennis G. if I could borrow his broom. He told me to be sure to put some gas in it before I brought it back. Did he think I was going to ride it? It wasn't even Halloween. Later, Margaret informed me that the nation's second most wanted criminal had been apprehended in the yard a couple of days before. It must have been a quiet arrest, as this was the first I had heard of it. If the FBI made the arrest, as they usually did in these cases, it was quiet. They didn't normally come in with horns blowing and guns blazing, not if they could avoid it. They had visited us before, always quietly. We never knew what distinguished personage might be camped next to us.

Although I meant that last sentence facetiously, there was some kernel of truth in it. At one time, one of Nevada's leading politicians (he still is) wanted to find out for himself what could be done to help the homeless people of the state. In order to accomplish this, Mr. Harry Reid dressed as a transient and spent a night at the Las Vegas Rescue Mission. He talked to as many of the other guests as he could. Rumor had it that only Reverend Compton, director of the mission, knew who the distinguished guest was. I did not recall what the politician's position was at that time. Today he is still a United States senator. He concluded that what would help many of the homeless people would be jobs.

Nevada has had and still has many good people in politics, to say nothing of the conscientious and caring leaders in other fields of endeavor than politics. After many years of being one of the country's more backward states, Nevada was struggling valiantly to come up to the twenty-first century.

Still later in the eventful day, an unexpected gust of wind blew my umbrella inside out. In sunny Las Vegas, I carried an umbrella to use against the burning sun more than against the rain. My friend Tommy used to call me Mary Poppins when he saw me coming down the street on a windy day with my umbrella at full mast. He said that any minute he expected to see me go sailing up into the air, ala the legendary Ms. Poppins.

It probably would have happened if my sunshade hadn't turned inside out before I reached the soaring point. We got some fierce winds in this valley. Some people laughed at me for carrying an umbrella in the sun. "Is it raining, Mary?" they gibed. My standard reply was, "No, but its sunning." That answer did not seem to impress my tormentors very much. They just went on laughing. Let them laugh; I did not get sunstroke when I was waiting in the sun, with the temperature at 110 degrees in the shade, for my bowl of soup.

Tommy had worked as a cowboy in his younger days, and he had many anecdotes about his life on the range. He was also very witty. I would always remember the twinkle in his eyes, when he was telling one of his stories. If Tommy were here now, I could probably write another book comprised only of his tales. I have not seen him for many years, and the last time I did see him, his health was not good. He was not his usual cheerful, teasing self. It was difficult to keep track of even our dearest friends out there. We did not have an address or telephone number, nor even know how to contact family members, to find out what happened to a friend. Many people did not want their families to find out that they were living like that, so we would have to be careful, even if we did know those things.

Tommy's story was about a young cowboy, newly arrived from the East, and unfamiliar with western flora and fauna. It was a classic. One dark, windy night, the young dude rushed breathlessly into the bunkhouse with a wild tale about being chased home by a ghost. Curious to see if they could find the phantom, the skeptical cowboys went out early the next morning for a look around.

What they found was a giant clump of tumbleweeds resting serenely and securely in a fence corner. Apparently, driven by a strong wind, the bushes had lived up to their reputation as travelers and followed the terrified young man all the way home.

I did not know whether or not Tommy's story was true, but I had no problem believing that it could be. I recalled a time when one entire lane of Main Street in downtown Las Vegas was blocked by a large clump of tumbleweeds. They were probably deposited there by the strong wind, which had blown through the valley the night before. I did not hear that "ghost" chased any startled motorists down the street, but anyone driving along Main Street at that time must have done some fancy ducking and dodging. That bunch of weeds was almost as big as the average car.

It might not have been a ghost, but it was definitely a traffic hazard. What baffled me was the fact that a road crew from the city had not removed the threat to life and limb before I saw it. I knew it was not just an old cowboy's tall tale since, as said, I'd seen that phenomenon for myself.

One spring day, when St. Vincent's dining room was still located on south Main Street, Tommy and I chanced to leave the building at the same time. As we walked toward town, a colony of ants bustling around in the dirt between the sidewalk and the street caught Tommy's attention. He paused for a moment to watch them. Then as we proceeded on our way, he said, "You know, the ants go by the temperature. When it's cold, they hibernate, and when it warms up, they come out."

March in Las Vegas that year had lived up to its reputation for being unpredictable. It was sunny and warm one day, then cold, windy, and sometimes rainy the next. Tommy had the weather in mind when he added, "Those ants must think the seasons are going by awfully fast." Even though I laughed, I sympathized with the ants. We never knew when we got up in the morning how we should dress for the day.

It is said that shared experiences bring people closer together, and we did a lot of sharing out there. We shared the blistering heat of summer and the freezing cold of winter. We shared the wind and the rain and the blowing dirt of the desert terrain. We shared our food, our cigarettes, and when we had any, our money. We shared our joys and our sorrows, our dreams and our disappointments. We were as close to each other as family—sometimes closer.

The beautiful flower of friendship blooms in even the unlikeliest of places. It pushes its way through the hard pavement of the street and makes life more bearable, which would otherwise be well unbearable. I don't believe that the people out there realized just how much their friendship meant to me. When the big, dark desert night was closing in around me and the other residents started leaving the compound for their night's camp, it really came home to me. I had no home. We had the yard during the day, but at night, there was no place to go but to a none-too-safe hillside, or a trash-filled vacant lot or field. Out there, we had no protective walls around us, no arcade roof over our heads, and no restroom conveniently nearby. We were outdoors, period!

We would be awakened in the middle of the night by flashing lights from a police car and a brusque command over a bullhorn. "Wake up, folks! You can't sleep here. Go to the desert area across the street, but stay out of sight." It is not an experience designed to make us feel at home in the world, either. It is no wonder one of the hymns most frequently requested in the missions was the mansion hymn. Even though I had sung it many times, I do not recall all the words. This is not an exact quotation, but one phrase goes something like this: "I have a mansion just over the hilltop." That was the dream of the homeless.

It was when I was making up my pallet on the ground, like some stray animal, that the depression, which bordered on panic, would all but overwhelm me. That was when I most often wondered how much longer I could take the stress and the degradation of the homeless condition. So many times I have been lifted from this deep, dark abyss of loneliness and despair by someone trundling past with his or her cart and a cheery, "Goodnight, Mary. Have a good one." Sometimes it was one of my neighbors starting the old Walton family "Goodnight" routine. Then we would all laugh. For the rest of that night, I did not feel so lonely, so scared, or quite so worthless.

In the winter of 1991–1992, I was very ill with the flu again. For several years, the winters in the valley were unusually cold and damp. My body reacted as it normally did to that kind of weather. This was not what I had come to the Southwest for. That winter, I was so sick that for a couple of weeks or so, I could hardly get around. One morning, when I was beginning to feel better, Dennis G. came over to wish me a good morning and ask how I was feeling. When I told him I thought I would live after all, he said, "That's good. For a while we (he and Hughie) didn't know when we would be picking you up off the pavement."

I hadn't known they were watching me that closely, but later Hughie told me that one evening, he had followed me to the Shade Tree because he did not know whether or not I would make it on my own. That was another occasion that I hadn't known of. Money could not buy the kind of friendship shown me by the other street dwellers. Those friendships will extend to the grave and beyond. Death cannot touch them.

Margaret had a somewhat different way of expressing her concern. One freezing morning, Margaret and I were chatting and shivering as we waited in the parking lot for the yard to be opened. I lamented the fact that I would probably live to be one hundred years old and still be living on the street. "Oh," the forthright Margaret replied comfortingly, "you'll probably die of a heart attack one of these days."

Only she could understand that I would rather be dead than live to be a hundred and still be on the street. For the past thirteen years, though, Margaret expected me to keel over of something or other. I don't think she particularly wanted me to die. She just didn't understand how I could live the hard life I did at my age without it killing me. I didn't understand it, either. Good genes, I guess, although I think my blood circulation would have been improved if I stopped smoking. Both my pocketbook and my opinion of myself would have been improved if I stopped gambling, or at least slowed down on it.

Anyway, because of those considerations, I supposed that Margaret, too, watched me more closely than I realized. I don't think that I could have written this book, modest though it is, without the moral support of my friends. If they had any doubts about my ability to write a passable book, they did not express those misgivings in my presence. Even those chronic skeptics, Margaret and Sarge, thought the book was a good idea.

It was all the more remarkable when one considers the fact that no matter what kind of an enterprise we had in mind, there was usually someone in the vicinity who was only too happy to throw a bucket of ice water on the idea. They listened for nearly three years to my cursing the rain, wind, heat, or cold—anything that would have kept me from writing. I would have wagered even my most loyal friends were hoping if I ever wrote another book, I would not be within earshot of them.

One evening, as we were waiting to get into the Salvation Army shelter, I reminded Margaret that for over three and a half years we had been living on cement surrounded by cement. There were no trees, no grass, no bushes, and no flowers, just cement. "Asphalt," Margaret corrected. Then she added, "The asphalt jungle."

I guess she was right, and I was awfully tired of it. It was not my idea of gracious living; more like, "Goodness gracious! Living?" But it was survival, and that was something; quite a lot, in fact. There was always the hope that things would get better if we could just hang on long enough.

We women owe St. Vincent's and the St. Vincent's coordinator, Mr. Dee, a lot of thanks for giving us shelter that year. After the Salvation Army terminated their emergency shelter program and told us not to try to get back in before November (their usual six-months waiting period), we were back in the arms of despair with no place to go.

When Nita and I called on Mr. Dee that day and told him of our dilemma, he seemed quite surprised. He got on the phone to the Salvation Army immediately and chewed out somebody for not letting him know that they were ending their program at that time. He could not, however, talk them into changing their mind. So he agreed to accept the women into the St. Vincent's shelter on an emergency basis. Those were the only terms under which he was allowed to accept women.

Had it not been for Mr. Dee, we would have been outdoors and out of luck. From what I had been hearing, Metro was cracking down on people caught sleeping outdoors. After all, we had all those shelters, didn't we? I didn't think my frazzled old nerves could take much more of that kind of treatment.

CHAPTER 18
THE LANGUAGE OF TOLERANCE

Living out there gave me a lot of time to think. Looking back over my life, I found that the times I regretted the most were those occasions when I may not have been loving enough and not understanding enough of other people. If I had one overriding motto, it would be: "Be loving." I might have occasionally done something foolish, but I seldom did anything hateful.

It would be nice if all the people in the world spoke the same language: the language of tolerance. We might not love each other, we might not even like each other, but tolerance would be a step in the right direction. I could imagine us looking back on the world, from the other side of the Great Divide, and asking ourselves incredulously, "Good heaven, was **that** what we were fighting over?" Perhaps we should ask the question now, before it is too late.

The longer I lived in this world, the more firmly convinced I became that the only legitimate use for power was to serve others, not to oppress and abuse them.

On July 22, 1992, somebody up there must not have liked the Shade Tree; or perhaps it was somebody down here. Whatever the case might be, once again a runaway car bolted down the Main Street hill and crashed into the exact same spot where another car had made its surprise visit to the shelter. That room was now the family dormitory, housing mothers and children. Some bricks were pushed out of the wall and some lockers were knocked over, but none of the residents were injured.

A guardrail really should have been put up outside that spot. It seemed to be particularly vulnerable to the onslaught of runaway vehicles. If one of the women had been getting into her locker, or if some of the children had been playing near the lockers, someone could have gotten hurt. Not even a brick wall could have stopped that car. It might have slowed the car down a bit, as only part of the automobile had made it into the building this time.

One day, Mike Raddig and I were discussing the art of writing. I remarked that I must not have been a very good writer because I did so much re-writing. Mike told me not to feel badly about it, and that we were in good company. As an editor, Mike did a lot of re-writing, too. He went on to say that Ernest Hemingway had once written some of the paragraphs in one of his books seventeen times before he was satisfied with them.

If it was good enough for Hemingway, I guess it was good enough for me. However, I felt I had written this modest little book seventeen times already, and I still didn't feel satisfied. It was not "War and Peace" or "Gone With The Wind," and it certainly was not Hemingway. If I ever decided to write anything really monumental, eternity itself would not give me time enough to finish the job.

I suppose this had been a particularly difficult task for me because I did not find this kind of a life to be at all interesting. As far as I was concerned, except for my friends and the excitement of gambling, this had been one long, dreary drag. Granted, gambling was a negative way to handle any situation, and it was an expensive pastime, too. Yet, one needed to get away from it all once in a while or go stark raving mad. Other people felt that way, too. At least that was what we gamblers told ourselves.

Speaking for myself, I would rather be dead than

bored, so I tried not to bore others in either speaking or writing. This sometimes took some doing.

There had been occasions of discouragement and despair when I felt like throwing my manuscript into the nearest dumpster and calling it a lifetime. But Hughie believed in me, and so did others. How could I disappoint my loyal friends?

People have brought me all kinds of articles they found while hunting cans or "dumpster diving" (looking in dumpsters to see what they could find). Among their gifts were pens, paper, needles, thread, scissors, crochet hooks, and yarn, to name a few. The most comfortable shoes I had were given to me by a friend who collected cans. I threw away three pairs of new shoes that were not comfortable once I wore them out of the store.

Come to think of it, I had had a couple of negative reactions when I was writing, although not about the idea of writing a book. One acquaintance of mine—I do not call him "friend"—told me that if I was waiting to get off the street before finishing my book, I would never get it finished. He meant because I was never going to get off the street. *The nerve of him*! If it was the last thing I'd do on earth, I'd show him the next to the last thing. The last thing would have been to say, "I told you so," to that pessimist, and then I could die happy. If I ever got off the street, I probably wouldn't want to die; not for a while, anyway.

That was the most negative thing anyone had said to me since I made the mistake of telling Margaret the name I had chosen for her, which wasn't "Margaret." I had a dear, sweet cousin named Margaret—one of Uncle Alf's daughters—so that name had nothing but lovely connotations for me. I just felt that "Marguerite" would suit Margaret, with her dark, curly hair and a general personality.

She did not agree with me, however, so I went back through the manuscript and changed the "Marguerites" to "Margarets." That was the lengths I would go to in order to make my friends happy. It was probably because I considered it their story as much as mine. I might have been doing the writing of it, but they shared in the living.

Hughie, by the way, wanted me to use his real name. He was getting such a charge out of being in a book. He wanted everyone to know about it. He was also my collaborator. He dug up the details of stories that I could not have gotten. He also gave me his support in other ways.

One afternoon, as Sally and I were walking down the hill from our four o'clock dinner at the Salvation Army, we were talking to a young veteran of the Persian Gulf War. He was only twenty-three years of age. He told us that he had been a member of an airborne unit; I suppose that translated to "paratrooper" because he liked to jump.

One day he had to jump from a plane that the Iraqis were firing on. That experience would have cured me instantly of any desire to leap from a plane, but not that intrepid young warrior. Even though he was so badly injured in hand-to-hand combat with an Iraqi soldier that he was on disability, he still liked to jump.

Until I heard some of those real-life stories, I had forgotten what it was like to be young, adventurous, and incredibly brave. Not that I was ever so incredibly brave, but those men were and still are. This man told the same story that we had heard from others; the story about the Iraqis who wept with relief when the Americans captured them. They wept, not because they were not brave, but because they were hungry and they knew the Americans would feed them. I would wager that Hussein and his family did not go hungry.

The Persian Gulf War was brilliantly planned, faultlessly executed, and a conflict of comparatively short duration. Except for those who lost loved ones, the victory seemed almost easy. From all accounts, however, the fighting must have been fierce. That war did not need much time to wreak havoc. The reports that we heard on television or read in the newspapers about the number of veterans on the street were sadly all too true. They were living proof of the price that some Americans paid for the freedom that we've all enjoyed. They were also a constant reminder of the debt that we and the people of other nations owed to them and their fallen comrades.

Another veteran I met in St. Vincent's yard, although he was a visitor and not a street dweller, was a veteran of the war in Vietnam. He was a doctor, not a soldier, but he had been a POW and was beaten so badly that his mind had snapped. At the time I met him, he was still trying to recover from that ordeal. I hadn't heard from or about him since that time, but I hope he made a full recovery both physically and mentally.

Two nights ago, I had a conversation with a paratrooper. This man was a seven-time decorated veteran of the Vietnam War. He twice broke his legs jumping from helicopters. His ankles were permanently damaged, but he still liked to jump. I could understand the thrill and the adventure of jumping from planes, but I thought that jumping out of a plane (right in the bared teeth of a shooting war) would be a bit more thrilling and more adventure than I could handle. They were not ordinary people; they were heroes. That was another breed altogether.

This veteran spent two-and-one-half months as a POW. He did not go into the details of that experience, but it was the touchstone for everything that had happened to him since. On the night we met in the smoking area outside the annex shelter at St. Vincent's, my new friend had been hit on the head a few blocks from St. Vincent's. Among other things that were taken from him were his shoes and socks. He was walking around in his bare feet until the men's clothing room opened the next morning.

He was furious at that treatment. He said no one had laid a hand on him in sixteen years, and then it took two men to do it. He recognized the man who had done the job on him while the other man held him. He had a very unpleasant experience in mind for that person. He also kept saying that he could handle this; it was still better than a POW camp.

CHAPTER 19
A NIGHT I WOULD NEVER FORGET

One Sunday morning, we were sitting in the parking lot as usual with our belongings piled around us. During the week we did our own cleaning, but on Sundays, we had to move out while a clean-up crew from St. Vincent's cleaned and disinfected the yard. Two of the men in my group were from Puerto Rico. Hughie said he had visited San Juan, and everybody there seemed to be named Juan (the waiter). The busboys all wore nametags saying "Juan."

The man who was parked next to us could not resist the temptation to make a pun. "When you've seen Juan, you've seem them all," he quipped. I wasn't the only punster in the yard, nor the best one. I'd let that chance slip past me, but not our neighbor.

I thought of a pretty good pun to put in the letter that I would enclose with my manuscript when I sent it to a publisher. It would be my luck to get an editor who hated puns.

On March 25th, we heard that Dennis G. had passed away suddenly of a heart attack. He had been stricken while he was away from the yard. We didn't ordinarily worry if people were away for a few days. They could be visiting friend or relatives, be on a drinking or gambling spree, or they might have taken a room to get off the street for a while. Dennis had been seen in the neighborhood, apparently in good health, so we were not expecting him to depart this world quite so soon.

I had known Dennis for several years; we had

worked in the dining room at St. Vincent's at the same time. It didn't seem possible that I would never see him again, or hear him consign me to outer space. Now, who would urge me to take the next flight to the moon—one way? Not Hughie—he was too much of a gentleman—and not Margaret. Her favorite question when people irritated her was, "Why don't you run away from home?" She didn't say to where.

Do we ever get accustomed to people simply disappearing from the face of the earth, never to be seen or heard from again? I was nearly eighty years of age, and I never seemed to get used to the phenomenon, as natural as it was. Maybe I just grew old without growing up, as Dennis G. might have pointed out. Dennis, I missed you, caustic wit and all.

The night of Friday, February 26, 1993, was a night I would never forget. I imagined there were others who would not forget it, either. The night was dark, cold, and rainy. It was a really miserable winter evening. People were looking forward, with eager anticipation, to getting into the shelter where it was warm and dry.

Those of us who stayed in the compound during the day had been given a few hours notice as to what was going to happen at the shelter that evening. But those who came to St. Vincent's only to sleep had no idea what was in store. As they started to go through the door of the annex shelter, they were told that they could come in, but if they were carrying any kind of a bag except a purse, the bag could not be brought in with them. Tote bags, shopping bags, purses large enough to look like a bag, backpacks, knapsacks, or even shaving kits were taken from them from that night on.

Whoever made that ruling had to know that they were homeless people; people who had no place to leave their small personal possessions and all they owned in the world. In answer to, "What will I do?" the shivering people who waited outside in the rain were told they could take their effects to the yard to see if someone would take care of the articles that night. Some of the people carried vitally needed medications with them. They could not afford to lose that.

Not only did many of the outsiders not know anyone in the yard, they didn't know where the yard was. They had to go across the large, dark parking lot in front of the main building where the annex was located. Then they had to go down Las Vegas Boulevard, past two buildings that were not connected with St. Vincent's, and then through an unpaved lot back to the yard. That night the lot was wet, muddy, slippery, and dark. It was difficult enough to negotiate if one knew the way, and almost impossible if one did not. There was a paved alley between the two buildings the yard residents knew about, but strangers would not know of it.

I don't know what some of the people did for shelter that night. I couldn't bear to think about it. Those who arrived at the shelter later in the evening were told that they could leave their bags in front of the guard's office in the yard and take their chances on something being stolen. Rather than wander around in the rain all night, some people did take that chance. From what I heard the next morning, some articles were stolen.

It had been some time since shopping carts had been allowed in the yard. The residents of the compound had to keep their carts on a corner, outside the fence, near the guards' office. Some of us had lost our possessions several times to vandals, thieves, or both. Eventually, St. Vincent's kept guards on the cart area part of the time, and that helped.

Originally, St. Vincent's took no responsibility for the carts. Friendship Corner made arrangements for us to park them in the vacant lot between the compound and Las Vegas Boulevard, and they maintained a watch over the area. Eventually however, some Las Vegans complained about the carts being so near the street in plain sight. Friendship Corner was also having a problem finding enough people to keep this vigil, so St. Vincent's gave us the corner by the fence.

Due to an infestation of insects in the shelter, we were no longer allowed to take our own bedding into the building. That was a rule the Salvation Army also had. They claimed that they cleaned the blankets every day, but that would be virtually impossible. Now at St. Vincent's, it was the shelter blankets or nothing. I had heard some of the men say they had seen a number of the shelter blankets being thrown into the trash because of their bugginess. I was one of those who decided to eschew her blankets. Instead, I slept on a bare mat using my coat for a cover and my purse for a pillow (not a very comfortable arrangement). I just prayed that the mat was not infected.

For several years before this new order, I had solved the sanitation problem by carrying a large, tough piece of plastic with me and placing it on the mat under the blanket. This protected me from the mat, and the mat from me. Now I was no longer allowed this protection. I didn't know what the answer to dirty shelter blankets was. Throwaway blankets, like throwaway diapers, would have done it, I suppose. But that would have been prohibitively expensive. I guess the best solution there was to get out of that kind of situation, if possible, and stay out of it.

From time to time, rumors that the yard was about to be closed rose to the surface. Occasionally, something happened that seemed to lend credence to those rumors,

naturally much to the consternation of the yard inhabit-
ants. At one point an announcement was made to the yard
people that refreshments were being served in the conference room for all those who cared to partake. Quite a
number of people accepted the invitation and hastened to
the conference room located in the central building.

Soon after they left, however, cart collectors, com-
missioned by one of the local markets to round up its stray
shopping carts, came to the compound. They looked for
the subject carts and when they found one, the possessor
was requested to remove his possessions and relinquish
the cart to the collectors. If the person using the cart was
not present, the collectors simply dumped the contents
of the cart on the pavement and took the cart. This went
on for a few minutes, and then the collectors got tired of
the work. After telling the St. Vincent's guards that from
then on, St. Vincent's could empty their own carts, the
disgusted workers left, taking a load of carts with them.

Normally, the people who had lost their carts would
have gone to the neighborhood metal recycling center.
There were usually plenty of empty carts there, brought in
by the can collectors. They had sold their load of cans to
the center and had left the empty carts. On this day, however, someone from St. Vincent's called the owner of the
center and had asked her not to allow the people from St.
Vincent's to get carts from her yard. She complied with
their request by locking the gate to her property.

Unable to get carts, some people lost some of their
possessions while the unprotected articles were lying on
the pavement. From that time on, whenever a visit from
the cart collectors was expected, a St. Vincent's guard
came through the compound to warn the people. I never
again heard of anyone from St. Vincent's calling the recycling center, either. Eventually, carts were barred from the
yard entirely.

We wondered how long it would be before people, too, would have reached the end of their tenure in the compound. Eventually, women were barred from registering for and occupying one of the numbered spaces into which the yard had been divided. For security reasons, women were not allowed to sleep in the yard at night. Now they could not stay in the yard during the day unless one of the men allowed them to share his space.

William did not stay around the yard during the day, so he allowed Margaret to occupy his place in the daytime. Hughie let me park my chair in his space with him. At night, we went to one of the shelters.

CHAPTER 20
A FAR CRY FROM THE ASPHALT JUNGLE

Despite the pessimistic prognostications of the erstwhile friend mentioned elsewhere in this book (I do not know where he was so I could look him up and say, "I told you so"), I did get off the street into a place of my own after all. In the fall of 1993, just in time for my eighty-first birthday, I got an apartment in the senior citizens complex in North Las Vegas, where I had wanted to live for a long time.

It is even more pleasant than I knew. My miniature dining room opens into a porch almost as big as it is. The porch, in turn, faces a park-like expanse of grass and trees, and one of the rose gardens, which gave this place its name. There were winding walks lined with charming, nineteenth-century lampposts, and the grounds are dotted with benches and lawn swings.

Early in the morning, the trees were luminous with the golden rays of the rising sun. It is like a scene from Fairyland—a far cry from the asphalt jungle in which I lived for so long.

My place is furnished mostly in "Early Friend and Late Thrift Store," as these apartments were not furnished except for the kitchen range and the refrigerator. I could not afford a furnished apartment and at these rents. I guess the Housing Authority could not afford them, either.

I decorated my walls, which are painted ivory white, with pictures that I cut out of magazines, newspaper supplements, and a picture calendar. Then I mounted them on construction paper, poster board or cardboard.

Now award-winning artists hang on my walls with beautiful paintings, whose works I could not otherwise afford.

Besides my homemade decorations, I also have a lovely original painting that my friend Esther found in the trash. The painting depicts a winter scene in a lightly wooded area. It looks as though an artist, who was a master with both color and the palette knife, did the whole thing with a palette knife. The painting is large, and it fits the west wall of my dining room as though it had been created for that very spot.

Several times a week for several months, I visited my friends in the yard, taking books, magazines, and newspapers given to me for that purpose. I usually stopped and chatted for a while. Until then, I had not realized how much I would miss those dear friends. Then suddenly, visitors were barred from the yard. After this restriction, I handed my literary gifts over the fence to whoever was around to take them. More and more the residents of the yard were being treated like criminals, except that even convicted and incarcerated murderers are allowed to have visitors.

I sometimes wondered if my friends missed me, as well as my attempts to brighten their lives with a little humor. I hadn't asked them, and they hadn't said. Usually they endured my efforts with patience, but sometimes they shooed me out of their camps. The last such occasion I remember was when I asked Hughie and anyone else within earshot if they had heard about the patriotic thief who refused to steal anything not made in America. I thought it was funny, whether they did or not.

Since I had not taken booze or drugs into the yard, and for months had not perpetrated a pun or told so much as a knock-knock joke, I could not be considered a disturbing influence. With that in mind, Hughie was able to secure the promise of a special visitor's pass for me. Before I found the time to pick up the pass from the office, the unthinkable happened; St. Vincent's closed the yard.

This action created quite a stir in the community of the homeless and among those who tried to help them. At the time, Mr. Tom Miller was the executive at St. Vincent's and over Mr. Dee. Representatives from the Homeless Advocacy Project and Nevada Legal Services hastened to the compound in an effort to talk Mr. Miller into keeping the yard open until something else could be worked out. They even offered to clean the yard restrooms, which were in truly deplorable condition. I attribute this largely to the fact that trash receptacles were not kept in the restrooms. When the women were in the yard, we tried to keep a cardboard carton in the ladies room for the trash. Most of the women used them, but the clean-up crew used to take the boxes away, and we couldn't always find a replacement.

On the day of the yard closure, which I watched on television, the man from Nevada Legal Services tried to get into the compound to talk to Mr. Miller, but Mr. Miller refused to open the gate to him. Refusing to give up without a struggle, the agent climbed over the gate. After further pleas from the determined Legal Services representative, Mr. Miller agreed to open the yard for a while longer. This agreement, however, must have been designed to get people off his back. Come nightfall, the compound was still locked up, and it has remained so ever since.

Now, some of the people were once again being chased from one vacant lot to another. Others, Margaret and Miss K. among them, found refuge at the Salvation Army complex, which now had a day room where men and women could stay during the day. I don't know what they did with their possessions, since there was now no yard to keep them in.

When I was "outside" and working on this book, I fully intended to end it with my getting an apartment, if I ever did. Until I saved the money to have the manuscript typed, however, I supposed I would have kept on writing because things to write about kept happening. First, there was the closing of St. Vincent's yard, and then Friendship Corner was discontinued. I was told that some women had complained about the men hanging around outside the building. Men have always hung around outside Friendship Corner, so I don't know what the big deal was. Perhaps some untold incident triggered the complaint, but if so, I did not hear about it. Anyway, Friendship Corner, with all its services to the homeless, no longer exists.

And would you believe another runaway car bashed the Shade Tree? According to the news report, this car also took out some power poles on its way to the shelter and created a power outage in that block for several hours. The broadcasts did not say that any residents of the Shade Tree had been injured in that accident, either, so once again, they lucked out.

One of my "moving in presents" was a television set. I was able to witness events like the implosion of the first of the Dunes towers in Las Vegas, Three Tenors in Concert, baseball, and so many informative programs. Television was indeed my window to the world. But of course there was "absolutely nothing good about television," Emory, as you claimed so long ago. Or has it been that long ago? Maybe it only seems like a lifetime.

Having a television also gave me the pleasure of watching events like the Olympics. I fell in love with ice skating that year, and Lillehammer! The very name looks and sounds like an enchanted city in a fairytale. For sixteen enchanted evenings, I was held spellbound by the drama of the people and the events in Norway. When the closing ceremonies were finished and the Olympic flame had been extinguished, I was suddenly and unexpectedly overwhelmed by feelings of loss and depression. What could possibly take the place of Lillehammer and the Olympics? Tears filled my eyes.

And I wondered about myself. Was I losing my mind, or was I merely being overly emotional? I got my answer the next day when I read a newspaper article in which Olympic withdrawal was mentioned. I knew then that I was probably not alone in my reaction.

Another Pearl Harbor day has come and gone. These anniversaries always bring back memories; memories of the years before Pearl Harbor, as well as the years after Pearl Harbor. Although there were not many of them, the years when I was a Navy wife were some of the most memorable times of my life. I loved the Navy then, and I love it today. I especially remember the spring of 1937.

Rollin and I had not yet separated. At that time he was stationed on the battleship Tennessee. That spring, the Tennessee was in dry-dock in Bremerton, Washington, for one of her regular overhauls. Some of the wives had joined their husbands in Washington that year. Several of the couples had apartments in a huge old house high on a hill, in a picturesque small town across Puget Sound from Bremerton. Port Orchard was its name, as I recall.

Our apartment was located on the front side of the building. As we sat in our dining nook, we could look out over the town across the water to Bremerton and the hills on the opposite shore. One morning, as we sat in our dining nook having breakfast before Rollin went to work, we looked out the window and saw another great battleship emerging like a giant gray ghost from the mist that covered the water at that hour of the morning. It was Big Mo, the legendary Missouri, also on her way to dry-dock. At that moment, I had no idea how sadly prophetic the ghost analogy was.

For years after Pearl Harbor, I had deep feelings of guilt and sorrow. I was safely back in Michigan instead of being in Long Beach when the battered remnants of what had once been a mighty armada, with her shattered crews, returned to their home base. I supposed some of them made it back. In Michigan, we did not hear much about the Navy, and I was both occupied and preoccupied with earning a living for my self and my daughter.

That time when the fleet came home, Rollin would not be with them. His remains were buried at Arlington. I have not been to Long Beach in many years, but I heard that the Seventh Fleet was no longer stationed in the harbor. Rainbow Pier and The Pike, too, were gone. I sometimes thought that I would like to live in Long Beach again. It was a beautiful city, and I loved the ocean and the beach, but it would not be the same for me now. I don't think I could bear the memories.

Every morning when I got up, I would look for the ships lined up on Battleship Row in the harbor, but they wouldn't be there. Neither would my apartment windows ever be rattled again by the big guns of the fleet. They regularly fired off their salvoes during training maneuvers, which were held some forty miles off shore.

That seems to have happened in another lifetime, so I force my thoughts back to the present and look onward to the future.

St. Vincent's yard and Friendship Corner are still closed. Hughie has worked off and on since the yard closed. Emory decided to go back to the ministry and talked of starting his own religious group. Bernie, too, decided to become a minister. I heard that he had moved to California. I will never forget Bernie, and I often wonder if he and Emory attained their goals. The others are scattered, and I have lost track of them.

It is Father's Day today, and I thought of a rather nice little habit that some of us in the yard had. On Mother's Day, the women wished the men a happy Mother's Day. On Father's Day, the men wished the women a happy Father's Day. We weren't gender confused; we just wanted everybody to be happy regardless of gender or parental status.

As I sit in my dining room on windy days, busily writing away, shadows form from the wind-blown trees in the courtyard outside. They make their way through the glass wall on that side of the apartment and dance ecstatically around the room. I feel like dancing with them. I can only wish that the stories of all my friends would end as happily as mine. They did so much for me; now I can do so little for them. I worry about them.

I still worry about my commas, too; so much so, in fact, that I went through this manuscript word-for-word again and deleted every squiggly little comma that did not look as though it belonged where it was. My "i" dots and "t" bars tended to fly all over the page, so I worked them over, too. At this point, I do not know which I am most: a writer, an editor, or a critic. I guess that a really serious writer needs to be all three.

Whatever I am, though, I have finally come to the very last words of this book. For the few pessimists who predicted that I would never get off the street and would never finish my book, I have only these words for them, wherever they are: "Nyah, nyah, nyah, nyah, nyah. I told you so, smarties!"

In Memoriam

Shortly after I moved into my apartment, I heard from a mutual friend that Margaret had gone into a rest home. Not long after that, I was told that she had passed away.

One sad day in May of 2005, Hughie also took his leave from Earth. Without Margaret and Hughie, "Pawn on a Chessboard" would not be the same book. In fact, it might not be at all.

Au revoir, my dear friends. As long as there is even one copy of Pawn lying around somewhere, you will live on in the world to which you gave so much, just by being a part of it.

The author

Tate Publishing, LLC

Tate Publishing is committed to excellence in the publishing industry. Our staff of highly trained professionals—editors, graphic designers, and marketing personnel—work together to produce the very finest book products available. The company reflects in every aspect the philosophy established by the founders based on Psalms 68:11, "The Lord gave the word and great was the company of those who published it."

If you would like further information, please call
1.888.361.9473
or visit our website at
www.tatepublishing.com

Tate Publishing LLC
127 E. Trade Center Terrace
Mustang, Oklahoma 73064 USA